Author

Vasyl Marchuk

SPECTRUM SLOVAKIA Series
Volume 49

Ukraine in martial law

Political and security challenges

PETER LANG **VEDA**

Bibliographic Information published by the Deutsche Nationalbibliothek
The Deutsche Nationalbibliothek lists this publication in the Deutsche Nationalbibliografie; detailed bibliographic data is available in the internet at http://dnb.d-nb.de.

Author: Vasyl MARCHUK
University of Trnava Faculty of Philosophy
and Arts Slovak Republic

Reviewers: Galyna ZELENKO
Doctor of Political science, Professor,
Head of Department of Political Institutions and Processes,
I. Kuras Institute of Political end Ethnic Studies,
National Academy of Science of Ukraine

Yuriy OSTAPETS
Doctor of Political science, Professor,
Dean of the Faculty of Social Sciences,
Uzhhorod National University

Anatoliy ROMANYUK
Doctor of Political science, Professor,
Head of the Department of Political Science,
Ivan Franko Lviv National University

ISSN 2195-1845
ISBN 978-3-631-93222-3   ISBN 978-80-224-2108-9
ePDF 978-3-631-93223-0
ePub 978-3-631-93224-7
DOI 10.3726/b22863

© 2025 Peter Lang Group AG,   © VEDA, Publishing House
Lausanne   of the Slovak Academy of Sciences
Published by Peter Lang GmbH,   Bratislava 2025
Berlin, Germany

www.peterlang.com   www.veda.sav.sk

Contents

Introduction

Today, humanity is experiencing large-scale transformations. They cover almost all spheres of social relations. Thus, it is important that the impact of climate change factors has increased, new dangerous diseases have spread, anthropogenic load on the environment has increased, the rapid development of the Fourth Industrial Revolution and active dematerialization of production. The global security environment is characterized by a high level of turbulence and unpredictability, the international system of strategic stability is collapsing, competition between states is intensifying, new conflicts arise, which are becoming increasingly difficult to resolve, including by military action. An effective response to the challenges of our time can be strengthening national security and ensuring martial law. The formation and implementation of state policy of the appropriate direction make it possible to effectively resist threats of any origin and nature, including hybrid ones, adapt to sudden and unpredictable changes in the security environment, and maintain the stable functioning of the state during and after a crisis and for a quick recovery to the optimal state of certain conditions of the equilibrium level. In general – to withstand (sometimes even survive), to suffer as few losses as possible in very difficult (crisis) conditions that cannot be avoided.

This result can be achieved by ensuring the proper level of readiness of the state and society to respond to a wide range of threats and risks, timely identification of vulnerabilities that weaken security potential, adaptive management, effective anti-crisis management and interaction at all levels, creation of necessary reserves and alternative strategies, planning of measures and implementation of universal coordinated actions, dissemination of necessary knowledge and establishment of reliable communication, rational use of resources, etc., namely the introduction of martial law. All of these actions determine the directions and priority tasks of forming a system for ensuring national stability, which has yet to be formed in Ukraine. Currently, Ukraine is facing a number of threats of both external and internal origin. Of particular concern are hybrid threats, which are especially difficult to detect. Their coordinated and simultaneous implementation in various areas is very dangerous for both the state and society. Counteracting these threats requires significant financial, technical and human resources, the volume of which is limited in most states and especially in Ukraine, which in recent years has suffered significant material and human losses as a result of the aggression of the Russian Federation.

In modern conditions, the potential for the stability of the state and society as complex systems requires adaptive development and management. The system for ensuring national stability is designed to perform these functions. Some of its mechanisms are used in Ukraine. However, their comprehensive implementation based on a systemic approach requires certain changes in the formation of state security policy, improvement of organizational and legal support in the field of national security and public administration, reorganization of existing and emerging interaction, state – wide systems (civil defense, counterterrorism, medical care, social protection, cybersecurity, law enforcement agencies, banks, etc.), which ensure the necessary cooperation and synergy of security and defense forces, state and local authorities, business and civil society organizations, filling it with appropriate systemic mechanisms, taking into account the cyclical nature of key processes and factors of influence, as well as in connection with determining the effectiveness of the functioning of universal and special mechanisms for ensuring national stability, the features of the formation of appropriate state policy, etc. There is also currently a tendency to manipulate the concept of "stability" in the field of national security, when non-systemic measures are proposed in certain areas under the guise of ensuring national stability. The above aspects require proper scientific study, and the relevant theoretical knowledge requires further development, taking into account their high practical importance in modern conditions.

The object of the study is the formation and implementation of state policy in the field of guaranteeing national security within the framework of guaranteeing the martial law regime.

The topic of the study is the formation of the national security system of modern Ukraine in wartime.

The purpose of the study is to determine scientifically substantiated conceptual principles and optimal ways to ensure national security in modern Ukraine, taking into account successful foreign experience, which includes the practical application of the concept of martial law in the field of national security.

The implementation of this goal involved solving many tasks, in particular: to determine the essence of the interdisciplinary concept of security, its characteristics and manifestations; to characterize the features of implementing the concept of stability in the field of national security; to substantiate the feasibility of implementing a systemic approach to ensuring national security; to generalize the conceptual principles of the formation and functioning of the system of guaranteeing national security, to determine and characterize the main principles, criteria, processes and mechanisms of guaranteeing national stability of an interdisciplinary nature; to analyze the features of the formation of state policy in the field of guaranteeing national security; to systematize and characterize the main mechanisms of guaranteeing national security; mechanisms for comprehensive assessment of risks and opportunities, identification of threats and identification of weaknesses, adaptive management, complex organizational mechanism at many levels, etc.; to characterize the justification for the choice of the martial law model and the main parameters of the corresponding system; to summarize foreign experience in ensuring stability in the security sector in the context of determining the possibilities of its application in Ukraine; to analyze the changes that have occurred in recent years in the approaches of international organizations and individual states to the development of security, in order to identify opportunities for expanding Ukraine's cooperation with them, as well as the application of relevant recommendations during the formation and implementation of state security policy; to characterize the modern security environment of Ukraine and highlight the main trends in its development in the context of determining the prospects for the formation of the national security system; to analyze the current situation and summarize the most important problems of ensuring stability in the sphere of national security of Ukraine; to demonstrate the feasibility of creating a system for ensuring national stability in Ukraine, to present the author's vision of its promising model; to develop recommendations for determining the conceptual principles of Ukraine's national security, developing the main mechanisms of the system, forming relevant state policy, improving national legislation, etc.

Research methodology. The research was conducted in several stages. First, a review of the scientific literature and grouping of sources according to the main areas of research was carried out – the theory of complex systems, research in the field of sustainability, security research. Taking into account the need to describe and clarify the main system mechanisms and processes of ensuring national security, scientific works on the issues of risk assessment and management, identification of threats and vulnerabilities, formation and implementation of state policy, strategic planning, state administration, etc. were singled out and analyzed.

The application at this stage of such methodological approaches and research methods as analysis, synthesis, systemic approach, system-structural, structural-functional, ascent from abstract to concrete, induction and deduction, historical, logical, etc., made it possible to form the theoretical basis for further research, and namely: to determine the conceptual principles of the formation and functioning of the system of ensuring national stability, the logic of building a multi-level complex model and universal mechanisms for ensuring national security, the peculiarities of the development of state policy in the appropriate direction.

At the same time, some factors became the basis for clarifying the main definitions, establishing the elements and connections of the system, determining the guarantee cycle of national security, characterizing the criteria, indicators, levels of stability in the sphere of national security, characterizing the criteria, indicators, levels of stability in the sphere of national security, determining the guarantee cycle of national security. that they are interdisciplinary in the sphere of national security. nature and guidance and assistance in the preparation of this monograph to the Director of the Institute for Strategic Studies, Doctor of Technical Sciences, Professor, Academician of the NAS of Ukraine, Director of the Institute for Strategic Studies, Doctor of Technical Sciences. Political Sciences, Professor, Director of the NAS of Ukraine (2019–2021). The author is also deeply grateful to the reviewers. The author expresses special gratitude to his family and friends for their support and inspiration, as well as to all the specialists who contributed to the publication of the monograph.

CHAPTER 1

Theoretical Principles of the Formation of Political and Security Challenges in Ukraine under the Conditions of Martial State

1.1. The concept of martial law in the field of national security: Research approaches to determining the content, structural elements, practical application

1.1.1. Research approaches to the formation of an interdisciplinary concept of martial law

The concept of martial law is disclosed in many scientific works. They concern various scientific fields and objects, in the context of which different definitions of this term are given, fundamentally different mechanisms of national security are proposed. Initially, this term was widespread in technical disciplines as a character-istic of certain physical phenomena and processes (for example, the ability of a material or mechanism to accumulate energy and withstand significant loads without destruction and damage). Lat-er, it began to be used in psychology (as one of the properties of an individual, which helps him not to change his behavior under negative influence), ecology (as the ability of ecosystems to recov-er after a disaster) and social relations. The concept of "martial law" is multifaceted, is used in different areas and has different shades of meaning. Other scientists argue that the existing defini-tions of the concept of martial law, its conceptualization and prac-tical implementation are not objective and are based on various assumptions.

This work is a study of the administrative and legal support of the legal regime of martial law in Ukraine. The conducted re-search is based on the analysis of regulatory legal acts and sci-entific works in this field. The work shows the features of the ad-ministrative and legal support of the legal regime of martial law. The concept of "martial law" is characterized as a component of the legal concept of state security, as well as its role in the practi-cal provision of national security. It is established that the main purpose of declaring martial law is to create conditions for the exercise of powers by state authorities, military administration, local self-government, enterprises, institutions and organizations in the event of armed aggression or the threat of an attack that threatens the independence of the state of Ukraine and its territorial integrity. Similarly, the introduction of martial law may be accompanied by the mobilization of human and material and technical resources in order to effectively and economically justify the resolution of the crisis situation, eliminate potential dangers and conditions contributing to their occurrence. The work analyzes the foundations of legal regulation of the introduction, operation and termination of martial law. In addition, attention is paid to the mechanisms for ensuring order and monitoring compliance with guarantees of citizens' rights and freedoms during martial law. It is determined that the administrative and legal support of the legal regime of martial law, introduced in Ukraine in the context of the aggression of the Russian Federation, is a complex and multifaceted activity. This process includes the study and application of scientific approaches, the development of legal mechanisms and the solution of practical tasks aimed at ensuring the effective functioning of state structures and maintaining national security during a crisis. The results of this study of the administrative and legal support of the legal regime of martial law in Ukraine can serve as the basis for further research in the field of military law, state security and legal regulation of emergency situations.

Interest in this topic is determined by the various approaches to the content and internal characteristics of administrative-legal regimes available in the science of administrative law. In the structure of the regime, numerous elements are traditionally distinguished, which most fully characterize its essence. The first element, the object-bearer of the regime, which can be: legal entities (regime of foreign citizens), social institutions (regimes of education, transport services), social processes (regime of economy, work and recreation), objects (regime of radioactive materials, documents of limited use), territories (state border regime, state of emergency, martial law), legislation (administrative law regime). The list of objects carrying regimes is not exhaustive and develops in two directions: toward the formation of new regimes or further specification of existing ones. That is, on the one hand, the prerequisites for functioning, the conditions that the environment creates for the regime bearer, on the other hand, the requirements for the regime bearer, the degree of his activity, the level of responsibility for the performance of his function.

This structural concept, generally supported by the author, however, has certain positions that require clarification and specification. In particular, in the legal literature, we find an opinion on the need to limit the circle of regime bearers to only subjects capable of conscious volitional activity and bearing responsibility for it (citizens, organizations, etc.). The author justifies his position by the fact that it makes no sense to attribute inanimate objects, phenomena, and social institutions to the bearers of the regime. Not fully agreeing with this judgment, we note that, having its specific purpose – to organize certain social relations – legal regimes can perform a regulatory function in various spheres and industries, including at the level of individual social institutions.

The second element of the structure of the martial law concept – the environment – is not without controversy. Understanding the environment of the regime as a certain set of external factors, in the structure of which there is an object-carrier of the regime and in relation to which this regime is established, in a number of cases it is necessary to investigate the issue of distinguishing the environment of the regime from the object-carrier of the regime. Most often, this is necessary in the implementation of regimes, the carriers of which are certain social institutions.

The content of the regime includes the set of means, methods, forms used for this purpose and the special order of their application to achieve the established goals, as well as the principles and rules of the implementation of this activity.

The structure of the sectoral legal regime, which is fully applicable to administrative-legal regimes regarding the concept of martial law, deserves attention.

1. The method of legal regulation, that is, a specific method of legal influence, characteristic of the industry.
2. Special legal means of regulation – prescriptions and forms relating to the ways in which rights and obligations arise, means of legal influence, methods of protecting rights, procedural forms, etc.
3. Principles, general provisions, that is, ideas characteristic of this field, general provisions characterizing its content.
4. A special branch of legislation headed by a codified act. The most important thing in this point is the presence of a meaningful general part, in which industry principles, general provi-

sions, and basic legal instruments are normatively fixed. The presence of a common part, albeit an external one, is a fairly clear indicator that the set of norms forms an industry, its uniqueness and place in the legal system.

A number of authors believe that one of the elements of the structure of the legal regime determines the goal, for the implementation of which a "special order of legal regulation" is introduced, namely: the goal of the legal regime is the unhindered realization of their interests by the subjects of the law. In general, the indication of the purpose of the legal regime is characteristic of many modern interpretations of this concept [22]. Vasyl Marchuk in "Ukraine's European Integration in the Political Dimension of Central and Eastern Europe" states that Eastern European enlargement has become a huge process for the EU system. Beforehand, the EU negotiated integration with small number of candidates at the same time, and if previously the processes of enlargement and deepening alternated, now they took place in parallel [75, p. 31]. The level of influence of public participation should be an adequate level of social significance of a project that the government plans to implement. Otherwise, the state does not influence on social tensions in communities and society. The government must constantly create opportunities for public access to comprehensive information on government plans and actions, as well as real mechanisms and further actions of the public. It is true to confirm that the participation of citizens in the management of public affairs in democracies cannot limit their participation in elections [75, p. 40]. The civil society of Ukraine is moving to a new, more effective stage of its development. Quantitatively designed, it begins to realize its potential and use it. This process will be an important step in the democratization of the country and during European integration process . Another important direction of the establishment of civil society is the overcoming of legal nihilism in society and the legal establishment of personal principles at all levels of public and state organization [75, p. 69].

It is impossible not to notice the variety of approaches to the formation of administrative and legal regimes and the identification of their elements. The list of structural elements of administrative and legal regimes includes the generally recognized part, with some exceptions. In this case, purposeful human actions are important, since within the framework of the concept, adaptation is associated with measures that support the development of the system along the current trajectory, and transformation consists of transferring development to other new paths or even in creating in such ways. Based on the analysis of various methods of research into the content of the interdisciplinary concept of martial law, it can be concluded that it is built around the ability of complex systems to respond to negative influences without losing their functionality and development potential. Given that the manifestations of the concept in different areas may be different, for the purposes of this monograph it is necessary to analyze the features of the implementation of the concept of martial law in the field of national security.

Vasyl Marchuk and Vasyl Dudkevych emphasize several trends of Ukraine's ability to become part of European Union:
- Ukraine has always been identified as a European state that, for some reason, has been determined for a long time with its priorities and implements them;
- Until 2014, Ukraine was inextricably linked with the Russian Federation, which affects the level of freedom in Ukraine's formulation of the same state priorities;
- the feeling of the Russian threat forces European countries to look at Ukraine's desire to get closer to the EU in a different way – as if this rapprochement strengthens the community's own security; and
- the described obstacles in Ukrainian-European relations are mainly reduced to the institutional inability to improve indicators of general well-being and the lack of political will. However, these shortcomings are not perceived as a critical safeguard of European integration, but only as a challenge to which Ukraine must respond [76, p. 44].

European integration and the development of civil society in Ukraine equally require the deepening of communication interactions, in particular social dialogue at the national, sectoral, and territorial levels, and the neutralization of barriers (artificial, external, resource) on the way to the promotion of democratic values. In the opinion of Vasyl Marchuk and Vasyl Dudkevych, it will be possible to solve the indicated communication defects, firstly, by informing about the available tools for including the public in the discussion of current European integration practices, and secondly, by giving the issue of European integration priority in the agenda of communication between the authorities and society, regardless of format and purpose of such communication [76, p. 107].

The existence of broad and narrow approaches to defining the concept of "administrative-legal regime" determines the same way of defining its structural elements. The author will consider different approaches to the content of administrative-legal regimes and, as a narrow approach, we will present the position of consideration of the elements of administrative-legal regimes, actually separate types of such regimes, in particular, the regime of legality of state administration, passport regime, state service regime, etc.

Researchers Yevheniy Haydanka and Marcel Martinkovič emphasize that more than 30 years of reforms in the former post-socialist camp countries, pose more questions than anticipated answers. The final transformation outcomes demonstrated diverse advances of these countries: from full European integration (e.g. Central Europe, the Baltic States, the Western Balkans) to a return and even strengthened centralized management (Russia, Belarus, Central Asia). Such a contradiction is a complex phenomenon caused by a group of factors, which may be the result of the approach of the political elite and the society to the management model [66, p. 14].

The model of decentralization of the Czech Republic reiterates the fact that decentralization can be the main solution to increase the political institutions' efficiency, providing better public control over political decision-making and overall high level of management efficiency [66, p. 114].

In the study of Marchuk and Dudkevych, it is argued that after gaining independence, Ukraine, in its vision of prospects, gravitated toward of the European way of governance and value orientations, and Europeanness as a civilizational marker inherent in Ukraine historically, geographically, and increasingly mentally. Ukrainians defended the development of the country during the Revolution of Dignity, and then on the eastern fronts, fighting back Russian military aggression. It is emphasized that to harmonize the purely spatial European affiliation with experience of democratic construction, to form an open competitive economy and parity relations with equal political partners – the content of the Europeanization of Ukraine's aspirations to find its place on international arena. The essence and content of the concept have been updated and categorized for Ukrainian political science "European integration practices," which the author defines as a functional component of European integration policy, organized according to the specific work plan of the state authorities regarding the implementation of European standards in all spheres of social life through the process of creating a regulatory and legal framework for integration, formation of appropriate structures for the implementation of political and legal decisions with the aim of acquiring EU membership. Practices are specific actions and decisions that are carried out in the institutional, diplomatic and extra-institutional directions. According to these criteria, Ukraine fulfills the conditions in real-time Association Agreements, improves national legislation, harmonizes the environment of relations with countries-neighbors and EU members, gains experience in democratization and constructive response to challenges and risks today. The importance of including the public sector in the progress of European integration is emphasized – representatives and organizations of civil society, which are both a driver and an indicator of positive transformations, and also perform the functions of a safeguard against possible abuses of power. Ukrainian civil society proved its ability to defend itself in crucial periods of state formation common national choice. The strategic demand of the topic of the dissertation research is argued by ongoing Russian aggression against Ukraine and acts of hybrid war, primarily its information war component (propaganda, disinformation). It is emphasized that, on the one hand, European integration can become a kind of reframing to strengthen the country's defense capabilities, on the other hand, the Russian threat is not only a Ukrainian problem, but also a security challenge for the whole of Europe, therefore consolidation of efforts for a common goal resistance is an urgent need for EU partners [77, p. 144].

The emergence of civil society is determined by the distinction between human rights (to life, the pursuit of happiness) and citizen rights (political rights). So, the most important prerequisite for the existence of both civil society and the rule of law is a person who has the right to realize both economic and cultural, spiritual and political potentials, realizing which, through civil society, a person reproduces social life. If a person is the main element of civil society, then his supporting structures are all those social institutions that are called upon to promote the full realization of the personality, its interests, and aspirations. Structurally, civil society is a dialectical unity of three main areas: political (relations arising in connection with the satisfaction of political interests and freedoms by ensuring the participation of citizens in different parties, movements, state and public affairs, associations) economic (economic relations, and before total property relations); and spiritual (the processes of functioning and development of civil society in the public and individual consciousness – in the form of scientific theories, concepts, as well as everyday consciousness, life experience, traditions) [78, p. 5].

Globalization processes taking place in the world have not only influenced and accelerated the development of the modern economy and various processes, as well as highlighted the problem new challenges and threats of the globalized polycentric world of the twenty-first century, but also actualized issues of adaptation of diplomatic services of states to the new conditions for strengthening the personnel potential, raising the level of professional training diplomatic personnel. Despite the fact that "interregional cooperation is an important aspect in the global system of international relations," however "the main actor of international politics and the most important subject of international law and will continue to be a sovereign state" [79, p. 2].

According to the concept being developed, the purpose of the military-political training of servicemen under contract as an educational discipline is the formation of competences in servicemen necessary for the performance of professional tasks of a political content, subjective images (personal meanings, meanings and relationships), which make up the cognitive basis of political consciousness of servicemen. The concept envisages the active inclusion of military personnel in the system of social relations and phenomena of the state's military policy. The selection of material is based on the general goal of training a specialist, the system of cognitive goals and the possibilities of the educational discipline. The concept is focused on the selection of leading, core concepts (ideas) in the content of the educational discipline, the definition of the main (invariant) core and the variable part of the content of educational modules. The use of "content nodes" of educational material (conceptual, ideological, subject-figurative, activity-based) allows for the specific creation of a monitoring and evaluation system aimed at checking the formation of the competences of contract servicemen in solving at set of educational and professional tasks. The developed concept is an indicative basis for solving the problems of developing the political consciousness of military personnel. The results of the study make it possible to find ways and means of developing the political consciousness of conscripts in a period of changing worldview priorities with respect to the professional education and training of military personnel.

1.1.2. Evolution of security research

The category of martial law security began to be considered a little later than other areas. This is due to the fact that the direction of scientific research in the field of national security was formed only in the second half of the twentieth century. The combination and mutual enrichment of research in the field of national security and stability occurred at the beginning of the twenty-first century. The term "national security" began to be widely used at the beginning of the twentieth century, as a result of an understanding of the role of the state in the system of social relations, methods of exercising power, and the protection of national interests. The development of the theory of international relations in the second half of the twentieth century, contributed to the intensification of scientific research in the field of national security. If national security is considered primarily in the classical realist paradigm of international relations, then national security issues are discussed in other paradigms – liberalism, the English school, strategic studies, critical theory, world studies, etc. studied within the framework of a separate direction of scientific research was identified – security studies in the second half of the twentieth century to the early twenty-first centurys a separate direction of scientific research was identified – security studies. Conceptual approaches to ensuring national security have undergone significant changes, as has the concept of security. After World War II, the traditional approach to defining security within the framework of the paradigm of political realism prevailed, according to which the main role in ensuring security was assigned to the state, and the main threat was considered to be external military, the possibility of danger . the origin of interstate conflicts is considered high, and the main role in resolving them is assigned to force. In addition, state security is practically synonymous with personal security, since it is a prerequisite for the well-being of citizens. According to R. Jones, such an approach is too static and limited. The events of the last decades of the twentieth century, in particular the end of the Cold War and the collapse of the USSR, did not suit him. At the same time, as the scientist noted, such radical changes occurred only peacefully. After the events of the aforementioned period, as predicted by E. Thompson, rapid and unexpected changes were to occur, including the breakdown of relations between states, as well as acute intrastate conflicts, which were "movement[s] without a map," as Thompson predicted. In the new conditions, a narrow (traditional) approach to defining national security, focused on the military component and state-centric in nature, needed to be revised.

The change in the security environment showed a wider range of threats and threats than the military one, and new non-state actors became more active in this area. For example, traditional research approaches neglected the consequences of rapid technological changes for security, especially in transport, energy and information. In such conditions, the theory of securitization, proposed by B. Buzan and other representatives of the Copenhagen School, was popular. The new research method made it possible to expand the content of the concept of security, including beyond the military, political, economic, social and environmental components. At the same time, the scientific community recognized the main role of the state in ensuring national security. R. Ullman, known for his research in the field of international politics and security, ignores the fact that interpreting the concept of "national security" only in the context of combating military threats distracts attention from non-military threats, as well as many aspects related to the protection of vital human interests.

Based on the conclusion of the 1994 Human Development Re-

port that world peace cannot be achieved if people are not protected in their daily lives, the priority of human security and the
new scientific concept of its components – economic security, food
security, health security, environmental security, personal secu-
rity, public security, and political security – were created. In general, in the early 1990s, security was provided by non-state actors:
citizens, society, ethnic groups, religious organizations, etc. Many
studies have appeared that define the role. In the field of scientific
expertise, the question of "security liberation" as liberation from
restrictions began to be raised. As we can see, the changes in the
interpretation of the concept of national security proposed by researchers in the mentioned period are aimed at increasing the
flexibility of the national security system. In addition, security issues began to be actively considered not only at the national level,
but also at other levels – regional and global.

With the emergence of the concept of globalization, the
strengthening of relations and mutual influences between them,
the emergence of new players in the international arena and the
formation of global networks, the debate about the role of nation-
states has intensified. The changes that have occurred in the world
under the influence of globalization have not made it safe. As
D. Held and A. McGrew note, as a result of the formation of a complex system of interstate political and economic relations, the national security strategy of many states is not much different from
the strategy of international security. The authors also argue that
globalization contributes to the transition from state-centric politics to a new complex form of multi-level management of global security. Although countries with different potential and levels of development have benefited from globalization to varying degrees,
there is a general trend toward a decrease in the ability to ensure
national security due to the insufficient institutional capacity of
nation-states. This has put on the agenda the issue of the need to
reform political systems at the national and international levels
in order to better meet the new conditions of world development.

It is also appropriate to pay attention to the discourse in which
nation-states (primarily world leaders) expand their understanding of security beyond the principle of protecting and promoting
national interests. The question of the need to protect possible human rights within the framework of the development of the theory

of the formation of a "global community" and the concept of the priority of human security. In particular, D. Chandler analyzed changes in the paradigm of security research and drew attention to this. However, the concept of responsibility for global security of "powerful" states and their right to intervene in the internal affairs of other states to protect basic human rights turned out to be more problematic in practice and created fundamental contradictions between law and the sovereign rights of independent states. In addition, relevant measures in the field of global security required adequate resource provision and became more burdensome for the national economies of "strong" states. Changes in the global security environment, as well as the emergence of new and strengthening traditional threats have actualized the issues of the imperfection of existing security systems and their incompatibility with new conditions. Thus, a question arises about the need for national security systems to acquire new characteristics that would allow states to independently confront threats and threats of various nature and origin.

The author emphasizes that security (in all its manifestations – state, national, economic, ecological, informational, demographic, etc.) is one of the most important categories of modern science and practice. Being the dominant activity of society, security cannot remain unchanged in various conditions of its transformation, therefore, its content needs constant clarification.

War is a phenomenon that crosses the boundaries of time, cultures and geographical coordinates, creating a unique environment where survival, security and the preservation of law and order become especially relevant. In this context, there is a need to establish and implement a special legal regime aimed at ensuring an adequate response to the challenges of military conflicts and preserving the functioning of the state in conditions of threats to public interests. It was these aspects that formed the basis of a scientific study devoted to the peculiarities of the administrative and legal provision of the legal regime of martial law. Martial law, as a special legal regime, is determined by a deep transformation of state functions, power structures and mechanisms of their interaction. It is a demonstration of the differences between regulated peacetime and the intensive mobilization of resources during armed conflicts. However, the introduction of martial law brings to the fore not only the issue of ensuring security and defense, but also the protection of the rights and freedoms of citizens during a state of crisis. Features of the administrative and legal provision of the legal regime of martial law include a complex system of measures aimed at ensuring discipline, order and preserving the normal functioning of society. Restoring or maintaining law and order in wartime requires a high level of organization, planning and coordination of actions from the state. At the same time, an important challenge is to ensure a balance between the restriction of individual rights and freedoms of citizens and the provision of their necessary needs in this important period for the state.

1.1.3. Peculiarities of applying the concept of martial law in the field of national security

The evolution of conceptual approaches to ensuring national security, the development of systems theory and the formation of a separate direction of security research (sustainable thinking) led to the spread of the concept of war in the field of security research and the emergence of the concept of war about "national security". Further understanding and systematization of relevant knowledge anabled the formation of an independent concept of national stability.

Investigating the formation and development of the concept of martial law, J. Walker and M. Cooper note that in the last decade the topic of stability has become widespread as an operational strategy for preparing for emergencies, responding to crisis situations and ensuring national security [40]. G. Lasconarias argues that the development of national security has become a very important task for states, as it allows them to prepare to confront new types of threats that became apparent after the start of the Russian Federation's hybrid aggression against Ukraine. In 2014, the war was declared in 2022. The position of K. Feder, the emergence of the concept of national stability on the national security agenda is associated with the expansion of the spectrum of new threats associated with the growth of global interdependence and uncertainty and the process of preventing military conflicts. In such conditions, ensuring security by the forces of nation-states becomes a very complex issue and requires new methods, in particular, the development of a national security strategy that accounts for the principles of ensuring national stability.

In the modern world, threats and threats to the security of a person, society and the state are growing and have acquired complex forms; it is practically impossible to prevent or overcome them. Counteracting such threats, as a rule, requires an integrated approach and joint efforts of various national security agencies. The implementation of the concept of stability in the field of national security is due to the need for a timely and effective response to a wide range of modern threats and crisis situations in order to prevent the development of destructive processes in the state and society. In particular, with their weakness or inability of the state to perform very important functions. In the context of countering hybrid threats, the implementation of an appropriate set of tasks becomes particularly relevant. They are characterized by the coordinated simultaneous use of a wide range of traditional and non-traditional methods and means of struggle in various areas, the active involvement of non-state actors. The use of complex methods of influence creates a synergistic effect. In addition, hybrid threats are often hidden in nature or disguised as other processes in the legal sphere. Therefore, such activities are difficult to define as a threat, especially at the initial stage.

These concepts are close in meaning but have different semantic shades and characterize individual aspects of certain processes or the state of a particular object. Thus, the concept of "state power" is primarily associated with its broad resource potential (as a set of material and spiritual capabilities used by the state to achieve its geopolitical goals) [19].

The International Organization for Standardization (ISO) introduced the concept of "organizational stability" as the ability of an organization to perceive and adapt to a changing environment in the "Security and Stability" section of the standards catalog [25]. According to the organizers of a study conducted by a group of Israeli and Canadian scientists, during which students from a number of universities in Israel and the United States were surveyed, the respondents' understanding of the essence of "national stability" was influenced by their individual perception of the main threats to national security, as well as a number of national characteristics and political and psychological aspects (in particular, trust in national institutions, patriotism, optimism, social unity, historical experience, cultural differences, etc.) [17]. In general, the differences between the definitions of "national stability" of Americans and Israelis according to the survey results were insignificant: the generalized American version was more abstract, and the Israeli one was broader. In a generalized form, the essence of this concept is defined as the ability of a nation to successfully resist threats (for example, terrorism, corruption, poverty, etc.) while preserving social values.

While in overall agreement with the conclusions of the aforementioned researchers regarding the content of the concept of "national stability," it should be added that the emphasis is on such definitions as nation, threats, social values, etc., which makes it possible to use an integrated approach in countering threats, crisis situations and other threats and defines individual functional characteristics (in particular, the preservation of social values). However, such a characteristic of national stability as "the ability to successfully resist threats" is too general and does not reflect all the characteristics inherent in the concept of national stability. It is primarily about adaptation, which allows the state and society to adapt to the constant impact of threats and rapid changes in the security environment, to work continuously in crisis situations and to quickly recover from the destructive consequences of any phenomenon/action. to the optimal level of equilibrium under given conditions [10]. Given the main provisions of the concept of stability in the field of national security, the author can say that the adaptation of the state and society does not mean a passive expression of the will of a more powerful subject of relations to the detriment of national interests, but a purposeful search for new formats and mechanisms for protecting national interests and realizing national interests, which will continue to work effectively in the face of threats.

Analyzing different definitions of the concept of "stability," taking into account alternative conceptual approaches presented in the above-mentioned scientific studies, determining what are the main features characteristic of the concept of "national stability," taking the meaning from other terms and forming the basis of the concept of national stability. In other words, in the above-mentioned definition of the concept of "national stability," the word "national" means belonging not to a specific ethnic group, but to a specific state (English nation state). At the same time, it not only reflects the processes occurring around the state as a political institution and its ability to resist threats, but also includes a wide range of social relations and objects. Summing up and taking into account the recommendations of the Alliance for Sustainable Development [34] on assessing the stability of complex systems, the author can highlight key problems, elements of the system and relationships. the concept of stability in the sphere of national security in Table 1.1.

Table 1.1. The main characteristics of the concept of national stability

The key question software of national security	Meaningful load	Meaningful load System elements and connections
Stability of what?	Object of sustainability	State and society
Resistance to what?	Destructive influences (stimuli)	Threats, crises, or actions against which the facility must be resilient
For what?	The goal of achievement stability and level stability	Adapting to a changing and uncertain security environment while preserving national values and protecting national interests
For whom?	Parties interested in receiving the appropriate result	State authorities and local self-government, civil society, scientific institutions, communities, the population are well protected
Who will do it?	Entities capable of ensuring the achievement of the appropriate result	State and local authorities self-government, civil society, scientific institutions, communities, population, which take certain measures to strengthen security and stability state and society

Source: Author's compiler.

Considering the above regarding the content and main characteristics of the concept of national stability, it can be argued that this phenomenon has systemic features. This is a description of the main elements of the system and the relationships between them – objects, subjects, goals, critical parameters, functions, management principles, etc., about being. The set of relevant elements and relationships forms a system of national stability. Such a conclusion is important not only for understanding the features of the application of the interdisciplinary concept of stability in the field of national security, but also for developing specific mechanisms and practical recommendations for the formation of state policy in the relevant direction. In the context of the above, it is advisable to analyze the features of ensuring national stability, the formation and functioning of the relevant system, to identify common features and differences due to which the system of ensuring national stability differs.

1.2. The martial law system: Essence, main characteristics

1.2.1. The essence of the national security system under martial law

As a result of the confrontation between "state" and "nation," legislation and comparative jurisprudence arose in the field of political considerations about national security, accompanied by the "dissolution" of the basic concept of "state security" in numerous modifications. National security – economic, food, environmental, religious, moral and ethical, security of witnesses appearing in court, etc. Thus, the primacy of personal safety over the safety of society and the state is actually proclaimed. With this approach, the interests of the individual determine the interests of society and the state. In addition, the state, from the point of view of liberal democrats, is unable to ensure the safety of the individual, as it is the main source of danger for him.

The main feature of the law is that state-legal principles permeate all three "blocks" – the individual, society and the state. Only the state can determine priorities, the relationship between different types of security, goals based on state interests. To clarify the essence of the concept of "administrative and legal support of the legal regime of martial law," it is important to reveal the main terms: "legal regime," "administrative and legal regime" and "martial law". In general legal theory, different authors consider the concept of "legal regime" from different points of view. In a broad sense, this term means the result of legal influence, that is, the state of social relations regulated within the framework of legal norms. This can be considered as an external manifestation of legal regulation in a certain sphere of public life. It reflects the dynamics of the development of legal relations, which is achieved by transforming all components of legal influence, including legal norms, acts of their implementation and application, legal facts, etc. In addition, it covers other legal phenomena such as legal awareness, legal culture and legal principles that interact to achieve the goals of regulation. In this context, the legal regime is an integral component of state and political regimes, which are formed and implemented using legal regimes [8]. In a narrower sense, the term "legal regime" or "regime of legal regulation of social relations" indicates a legal structure that determines the way of organizing legal influence in a certain sphere of public life. This structure is formed through a specific combination of goals, object, methods, techniques and types of legal regulation, which determine the development of legal relations in a spatial and temporal context, as well as their industry specifics [18]. In general, the concept of "legal regime" can be interpreted as a special way of organizing legal influence, which manifests itself in an appropriate combination of legal means and creates a certain social condition, which can be favorable or unfavorable for the satisfaction of the interests of legal subjects [6]. They determine the gradation of the severity of legal regulation, its impact on the interests of legal subjects and facilitate or complicate the realization of these interests depending on specific conditions. At the same time, the activity of the subjects of legal relations is considered, and the optimal level of their participation in this context is taken into account [20, p. 15–16]. Thus, in the opinion of T. P. Minka, "legal regime" is an external manifestation (legal form) of the mechanism of legal regulation in a certain sphere of social life [9, p. 185]. As for A. S. Slavko, his definition of "legal regime" includes a set of legal instruments, with the help of which a clearly defined area of social relations is specifically (as opposed to general norms) ordered, taking into account temporal, spatial or personal parameters [19, p. 6]. However, even in the light of various approaches to the concept of "legal regime," a common aspect emerges from the general features. This is a special legal order that is established for specific spheres of social relations or for society as a whole (for example, border regime, customs regime, regime in prisons, legal regime of land and property, regime of legality, etc.) [22, p. 325]. So, summarizing the above, the author can say that the legal regime is a set of rules, norms, procedures and restrictions established by legislation to regulate a certain social or economic phenomenon, state or relationship. This term covers the set of rights and obligations of subjects operating within a certain legal environment, and also establishes mechanisms for ensuring compliance with these rules and the consequences for their violation. The specified characteristics are, of course, characteristic of the administrative-legal regime, which can also be considered as a special order of administrative-legal regulation that creates the desired state.

Public administration through the introduction of its structures, tools and procedures, as well as the procedure for realizing the rights and freedoms of citizens and the rights and legal interests of legal entities. In the administrative and legal literature, this regime is defined differently: as a combination of administrative and legal means of regulation, which is manifested in a centralized order, an imperative method of legal influence and legal inequality of the subjects of legal relations [9, p. 282]; as a legal institution clearly prescribed in legislation, associated with a complex of legal means – principles, ways and methods of regulation, procedural forms of responsibility and protection [19, p. 263]; as a special form of legal regulation of social relations, which is based on a combination of a complex of legal, organizational and technical procedures and administrative and legal means and determines the extent of possible and appropriate behavior of subjects, gives a special orientation to social relations in the sphere of public power [22]; as specific means of legal regulation, among which prohibitions, orders and universally binding prescriptions dominate [5, p. 22]; as a set of rules of activity, actions and attitudes, the introduction of which is determined by the specificity of the subject of regulation, which consists in establishing a set of rules formulated in the form of permits, prohibitions, regulations, procedures, which must be followed by subjects of public administration, in order to ensure the most effective rights, freedoms, legal interests of individuals, rights and freedoms of legal entities, ensuring and maintaining the sovereignty and defense of the state, security interests and protection of civil order [9], etc. So, the author can summarize that the administrative-legal regime is a system of norms, rules, procedures and mechanisms established in the sphere of activity of public power and administration, in order to ensure regulation and control of the behavior of subjects in the sphere of administrative relations. This regime covers norms related to the activities of state bodies, administrative procedures, interaction between the authorities and citizens, and 302 No. 8/2023 establishes rules for resolving disputes and conflicts arising in the field of administration.

According to the law, the main subject of security is the state, which performs functions in this area through legislative, executive and judicial authorities. Subjects of security are also citizens, as well as public and other organizations and associations. In this legal aspect, the identification of "individual, society and state" as specific subjects of state security is fully justified. There is a single system of state security for all its subjects based on a single state policy in the sphere of security, which is achieved by the systematic application of economic, political, organizational and other measures adequate to threats to the vital interests of citizens, individuals, society and the state.

The Law "On Security" forms such a model of the distribution of powers between the legislative and executive authorities in the field of security. They must be united according to certain rules and aimed at a certain result of the functioning of the system, different (usually greater) than that which can be given by its individual elements or other systems. The analysis of the national stability system using a systems approach should take into account the following basic patterns: social phenomena should be considered as structural systems that create a stable unity of elements, their connections and the integrity of the system; a system is a set of interrelated variables; a system is characterized by system parameters – features by which it can be identified and classified; complex systems contain simple systems; complex systems are open, constantly interact with the external environment, their functioning corresponds to the goal, are able to solve the tasks of different groups, there are different levels of structural organization. In the further analysis, other patterns of the formation and functioning of complex systems will be taken into account. As in the national security system, the national stability system also needs a mechanism for its functioning and development, which would ensure the interaction of all its components, and the system began to produce the expected result. Its main goal is to carry out certain activities aimed at achieving the set goal.

The corresponding mechanism is integrated and structured, its elements are closely interconnected, in particular, it is a system for ensuring national stability with a common mission and goal. Violation of the connections between the elements of this system can lead to its damage or destruction. Ensuring its integrity and balance is influenced by direct and feedback links between elements, the nature of interaction with other systems, the influence of the internal and external security environment, etc. Therefore, the previously proposed definition of national stability and the system for ensuring national stability in the corresponding concept can be defined as a complex mechanism for interaction between central government and local government bodies, civil society enterprises, institutions and organizations. Targeted actions, methods, factors and mechanisms that ensure the security and continuous functioning of society, the population, as well as the main spheres of life of society and the state before, during and after the crisis, including through adaptation to the crisis, threats and rapid changes in the security environment.

The main stimuli (destructive influences) to which the system of ensuring national stability must respond are threats of various nature and origin, crisis situations and other threats. In this case, stimuli (input actions) can affect various elements of the system, but primarily on objects that determine the contours of the system and must have certain qualities with a given purpose. First of all, it is about the fact that various threats and crisis situations can have different nature and intensity of negative impacts on objects of national stability, deforming both their elements and systemic connections. However, the functioning of the national stability system is aimed at preserving the integrity of both objects and systemic connections, which allows them to perceive such influences, resist them, adapt to the influences without significant loss of functional capabilities, recover and develop after crises.

1.2.2. Characteristics of objects and subjects in the national security system

In general, objects of stability can be various objects (metals, structures, etc.), socio-technical systems (political, economic, energy, information, infrastructure, etc.), people, organizations, etc. As complex systems, they have a potential for stability that can be increased. The state and society as the main objects of national stability are also complex systems. Various threats can affect their elements and systemic connections in different ways, and therefore, the mechanisms for strengthening the stability of the state and society can be different. To identify specific mechanisms and practices that need to be used to strengthen the stability of individual components of the state and society, it is necessary to use a decomposition approach to these objects. In this case, it is important to take into account the general systemic characteristics of the main objects, their internal connections and interaction with other elements of the national stability system. In science, the listed types of national security objects are not supported by all authors. The state together with civil society constitutes society. In the context of national security, the environment is only one of the spheres of social life, the basis of which is social interaction. It takes place in any sphere of social life, diverse in content, but its basis is always intersubjective. Interaction in any sphere of social life (economic, political, environmental, spiritual, etc.), first of all, always has a social character, since it reflects the relationship (in the most general form) between individuals and their groups. Relationships determined by the goals, needs and interests that each of the interacting parties seeks to achieve, satisfy and implement.

Thus, from the point of view of the impact of incentives on them, the characteristic features of the objects of the national stability system are the scale of the corresponding impact and its connection with the state of national security. In the process of forming the stability of the state and society as the main objects and their subsystems, it is important to understand which of their elements/characteristics should remain unchanged in order to ensure their integrity during adaptation to changes in the security environment or the ability to perform a basic function that can be modified, supplemented or removed to achieve a specific goal and ensure development in difficult conditions. Often, researchers divide the national system of sustainable development into the following levels of organization: state, regional (within the state), local (level of the territorial community), and object (organizational stability). There may also be transnational systems of stability: regional (interstate) and global.

1.2.3. System communications in the field of ensuring national security

The interaction of subjects and objects is determined by a specific goal and is aimed at achieving such results as reducing the risks and consequences of crisis situations, ensuring the continuity of the state and society in various conditions, strengthening the stability of key areas objects and their components in relation to destructive influences (stimuli) of internal and external origin, in particular, strengthening existing systemic connections and creating new systemic connections, etc. The interaction of the main elements of the system for ensuring national stability and the external environment is schematically shown in Figure 1.1.

Note: SZNB is the national security system; SSU is a system of state administration.

Given the fact that elements of complex systems can be other systems that interact with each other, in the context of maintaining the stability of a complex system, according to the conclusion of one of the founders of the general theory of systems, protection from external influences and maintenance of internal connections are two manifestations of the same trends

Anticipation of changing external influences and preparation for them is a question not only of success, but also of the very existence of such systems. Organizations should distribute the capabilities they have in a balanced way: increase work in some areas and decrease in others. At the same time, in the direction where it is expected to weaken the resistance of the environment, it is advisable to use offensive tactics, and vice versa: where an increase in enemy activity is expected, it is necessary to strengthen the de-

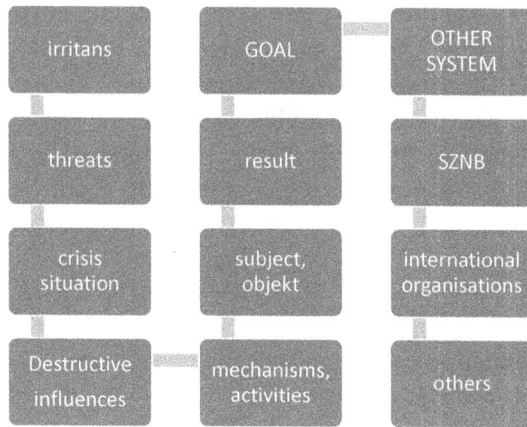

Figure. 1.1. The system of ensuring national stability in interaction with the external environment

Source: compiled by the author.

fense. Determining the nature and peculiarities of the formation of connections between the elements of the system, as well as with its external environment, increases the effectiveness of the formation and implementation of state policy in the field of ensuring national security and stability.

In general, the concept of "legal regime" can be interpreted as a special way of organizing legal influence, which manifests itself in an appropriate combination of legal means and creates a certain social condition, which can be favorable or unfavorable for the satisfaction of the interests of legal subjects [6]. According to the definition of "legal regime" is a system of interacting legal means based on general normative principles. These tools reflect themselves as a single legal structure that ensures a permanent normative design of a certain sphere of social relations. They determine the gradation of the severity of legal regulation, its impact on the interests of legal subjects and facilitate or complicate the realization of these interests depending on specific conditions. At the same time, the activity of the subjects of legal relations is considered, and the optimal level of their participation in this context is taken into account [20, p. 15–16].

The author can summarize that the legal regime is a set of rules, norms, procedures and restrictions established by legislation to regulate a certain social or economic phenomenon, state or relationship. This term covers the set of rights and obligations of subjects operating within a certain legal environment, and also establishes mechanisms for ensuring compliance with these rules and the consequences for their violation. The specified characteristics are, of course, characteristic of the administrative-legal regime, which can also be considered as a special order of administrative-legal regulation, which creates the desired state of public administration through the introduction of its structures, tools and procedures, as well as the procedure for realizing the rights and freedoms of citizens and the rights and legal interests of legal entities. In the administrative and legal literature, this regime is defined differently: as a combination of administrative and legal means of regulation, which is manifested in a centralized order, an imperative method of legal influence and legal inequality of the subjects of legal relations [9, p. 282]; as a legal institution clearly prescribed in legislation, associated with a complex of legal means – principles, ways and methods of regulation, procedural forms of responsibility and protection [19, p. 263]; as a special form of legal regulation of social relations, which is based on a combination of a complex of legal, organizational and technical procedures and administrative and legal means and determines the extent of possible and appropriate behavior of subjects, gives a special orientation to social relations in the sphere of public power [22]; as specific means of legal regulation, among which prohibitions, orders and universally binding prescriptions dominate [5, p. 22]; as a set of rules of activity, actions and attitudes, the introduction of which is determined by the specificity of the subject of regulation, which consists in establishing a set of rules formulated in the form of permits, prohibitions, regulations, procedures, which must be followed by subjects of public administration, in order to ensure the most effective rights, freedoms, legal interests of individuals, rights and freedoms of legal entities, ensuring and maintaining the sovereignty and defense of the state, security interests and protection of civil order [9], etc.

The author can summarize that the administrative-legal regime is a system of norms, rules, procedures and mechanisms established in the sphere of activity of public power and administration, in order to ensure regulation and control of the behavior of subjects in the sphere of administrative relations. This regime covers norms related to the activities of state bodies, administrative procedures, interaction between the authorities and citizens, and also establishes rules for resolving disputes and conflicts arising in the field of administration. Among the special administrative and legal regimes, it is possible to single out the regime that is introduced in the event of armed aggression or threat of attack, danger to the state independence of Ukraine, its territorial integrity, namely, the legal regime of martial law. The legal basis for the introduction of a special administrative and legal regime of martial law in Ukraine is the Constitution of Ukraine [2]; the Law of Ukraine, "On the Legal Regime of Martial Law," the Decree of the President of Ukraine, "On the Introduction of Martial Law in Ukraine" [16]; the Decree of the President of Ukraine, "On General Mobilization "[12]; the Law of Ukraine, "On the Defense of Ukraine" [15]; and the Law of Ukraine, "On the National Security of Ukraine" [14]. However, it should be noted that the system of legal acts, with the help of which the goal of introducing the legal regime of martial law is achieved, is not limited to those mentioned above. The specified system of normative legal acts also includes both the laws of Ukraine and subordinate normative legal acts.

Regarding the concept of martial law, it should be noted that it has received a legislative definition. According to Art. 1 of the Law of Ukraine, "On the Legal Regime of Martial Law" is a special legal regime introduced in Ukraine or in some of its localities in the event of armed aggression or threat of attack, danger to the state independence of Ukraine, its territorial integrity, and provides for the provision of appropriate forging society and ensuring security in conditions of heightened conflict [21].

The essence of the legal regime of martial law is revealed through the implementation of a set of measures activated during its period of effect. According to Article 8 of the Law of Ukraine, "On the Legal Regime of Martial Law," it is established that measures related to the legal regime of martial law can be implemented and controlled by the military command jointly with military administrations (during their existence), depending on the circumstances, independently or together with executive power bodies and local self-government bodies. In this context, the implementation of temporary restrictions on the constitutional rights and freedoms of individuals and citizens, as well as the rights and legal interests of legal entities, provided for by the Decree of the President of Ukraine on the introduction of martial law, is an important component of this process.

1.3. Theoretical principles of assessment and management of national security

1.3.1. National security criteria

The system parameters that can be used to identify the system of ensuring national sustainability are, in particular, the criteria of national sustainability and the principles of its provision. The stability of objects ensuring national stability is formed due to their acquisition of a set of necessary qualities – fundamentally important characteristics that allow identifying stability and distinguishing it from other states or processes inherent in the state and society. The methods of achieving the specified parameters determine the nature of the mechanisms for ensuring national stability, which enable the relevant system to fulfill its mission. In the expert environment, there are different approaches to defining the criteria of national stability, which is caused by different interpretations of the concept of national stability. One of the most important characteristics of the stability of any complex system is its adaptability – the ability to resist influences, adapt to changes in the environment thanks to certain internal changes, which allows the system to maintain its integrity and continue to perform its functions. In addition to the specified criterion, A. Uyemov also attributes its simplicity or complexity, its reliability, the stability of the structure, individual elements, and system connections to the system parameters related to the stability of the system [13]. J. Fixel, in turn, considers the following criteria of system stability: diversity (existence of many forms and behavior of the system); efficiency (functioning under the condition of economical consumption of resources); adaptability (flexibility to changes as a response to influences); cohesion (the existence of unifying forces or connections) [22].

It is impossible to fully understand the current relationship between Ukraine and Russia or the current military conflict in Ukraine without considering the history of Ukraine, its development and historical relations with today's Russia, which in the past have been very volatile. From a mutual relatively calm neighborhood, through alliances, vassalage, cooperation and mutual conflicts. One can come across an opinion that claims that today's Ukraine is an artificially created state that arose before the Russian Civil War in the early 1920s and was then completely artificially created by the formation of the Soviet Union and the ruling Communist Party led by Volodymyr Ilyich Lenin. These views claim that Ukraine has always existed only as a part of Russia and that is the only way it should continue to exist. This chapter explains why this is not the case and that today's Ukraine existed in some form before it became an ally, then a vassal, and then in some form part of Russia. Moreover, the territory that is currently internationally recognized as part of Ukraine was not part of Russia, nor were the state units into which Russia was gradually transformed (the Russian Empire, the Soviet Union, the Russian Federation), historically dominated for a long time and was rather a temporary possession than a real one part of Russia. It is important to remember that part of the region known as Galicia, which is located in the western part of Ukraine, with approximately one-half held by Ukraine and the other by present-day Poland, became part of Russia (Soviet Union) only in 1939. Thus, Russia's historical right to Ukraine, that is, to a part of Ukraine, which is voiced from time to time, is at least very vague. If we even consider that this is something like a historical right against the state is a legitimate reason for waging an offensive war. Summarizing the above, the main criteria of social stability should be defined as: criteria of the stability of the state of society/community: identity; coherence and unity; connections between different social groups; involvement of the population in economic, political and other activities within the state, community; trust in the authorities; criteria for sustainability of society/community functioning: effectiveness of community management; citizens' awareness of the nature and character of threats, as well as the procedure for actions in the event of their occurrence; readiness to respond; controllability of the situation before, during and after the crisis; creation of joint capabilities to confront a threat, a crisis. The classification of the basic criteria of national stability depending on the type of objects in terms of the main components of the state and society, as well as their condition or ability to function, which are the defining characteristics of stability in the field of national security, is given in Table 1.2.

The proposed methodology for determining the basic criteria of national sustainability is interdisciplinary in nature and can be used as a basis for the development of specific sustainability criteria related to various industries, objects and spheres of social relations.

Table 1.2. Classification of basic criteria of national stability

Objects	Sustainability criteria state of the object	Stability criteria functioning of the object
Branches, subsystems, technical complexes, organizations, processes, security system national stability etc.	• Reliability; • redundancy; • adaptability; • absorption	• Readiness; • speed; • response; • recovery
Society, communities, social groups, etc.	• Identity; • coherence and unity; • connections between different social groups; • involvement of the population to economic, political and other activity within communities; • trust in the authorities	• Effectiveness of management community/group; • citizens' awareness nature and character of threats and procedures in case of their occurrence; • readiness to respond; • controllability of the situation until, during and after the crisis; • joint creation capabilities for confronting a threat, a crisis

For an in-depth study of the resilience of various target groups (communities, organizations, the population, etc.) and industries to certain threats or destructive influences, detailed criteria can be developed that characterize the specifics of the selected group or industry and the peculiarities of its response to relevant threats and impacts (for example, criteria for the resistance of the rural and urban population to disinformation, the resistance of critical infrastructure objects to terrorist threats, etc.).

1.3.2. Factors influencing the formation of national security

The discovery of the adaptive cycle of the development of complex systems made it possible to determine the laws that determine the different effectiveness of the impact on the stability of complex systems in different phases of the cycle. The adaptive cycle alternates between slow and gradual phases of growth and accumulation, as well as shorter periods of reorganization that create opportunities for innovation. Intervening at different stages of the adaptive cycle can have different consequences for the development of the system. Thus, one and the same event (phenomenon, trend) can pose a threat to one state (for example, migration as an excessive burden on national social and medical security systems) and not pose a threat to another (for example, migration as an influx of qualified personnel to the domestic market), as well as be assessed differently in different time periods (for example, migration in conditions of sustainable development or armed conflict).

On the basis of the above, it can be concluded that the time factor and the context of the situation are variables that need to be taken into account in adaptive management in the field of ensuring national security and stability and the formation of state policy of the appropriate direction. In particular, it is important to establish and periodically review the level of national sustainability, including regarding individual subsystems and elements of the state and society, which can be considered sufficient under certain conditions. The influence of the time factor on the processes of determining the ways of development of the system determines the formation of permanent connections between the past, present and future.

Learning the lessons of the past, in particular taking into account the experience of overcoming the consequences of past disasters and crises, is important for building and developing the necessary capabilities to confront current and future threats, as well as to function effectively under conditions of chronic stress and uncertainty. For example, the mandatory investigation of the causes of air transport disasters in accordance with the requirements of ICAO (ISAO) is designed to increase the safety of air transport by eliminating possible deficiencies in the organization of transportation, aircraft design, personnel training, etc.

On the basis of the above, it is possible to draw a conclusion about the expediency of applying a comprehensive approach to managing the level of national security. First of all, it is about the need to periodically assess the stability of the main objects and their components for their compliance with the specified indicators in terms of the basic criteria of national stability. Even if the objects meet the specified criteria, the optimal and permissible level of national sustainability must be specified taking into account the results of the analysis of various influencing factors (time, context of the situation, etc.). In order to determine the measures necessary for adjusting the level of national stability and/or bringing the stability of the main objects and their components into compliance with the basic criteria of national stability, it is necessary to establish the phase of the adaptive cycle of the development of the state and society. This will make it possible to apply measures that will have the highest effectiveness in a specific period of time. In addition, it is advisable, if possible, to eliminate or minimize negative impacts on national sustainability from other systems.

1.3.3. The main processes, principles and mechanisms of ensuring national security

On the basis of the above-mentioned regularities of ensuring national security and the functioning of the corresponding system, it can be concluded that a significant part of the purposeful actions of various actors falls on the stage that precedes the onset of a crisis situation or the action of a threat (pre-crisis). During this period, preparations are made for a possible response to threats and crisis situations, the necessary knowledge and skills are disseminated, reserves are formed, and vulnerabilities are identified. Taking into account the features of adaptive management, the following should be singled out among the most significant processes in the field of ensuring national security that must be carried out at this stage: constant monitoring of the security situation; assessment of risks, identification of threats, determination of vulnerabilities, assessment of capabilities and level of readiness of various subjects to respond to threats and crisis situations; prevention

of threats, minimization of destructive effects and possible consequences of the implementation of threats and crisis situations,
elimination of the causes of conflicts; ensuring the readiness of
state and local self-government bodies, institutions, enterprises,
organizations, communities, civil society, and the population to
respond to any threats and crisis situations; event planning and
crisis management, in particular, the development of sectoral and
organizational resilience plans, the implementation of universal
protocols of coordinated actions in response to threats and crisis situations, and the restoration of the functioning of the main
spheres of life of society and the state at a level not lower than
the pre-crisis level; ensuring effective coordination and clear interaction of security and defense sector bodies, other state bodies,
territorial communities, business, civil society and the population
in preventing and responding to threats and crisis situations and
overcoming their consequences; acquiring and spreading the necessary knowledge and skills to ensure safety and stability; establishing and maintaining reliable channels of communication between state bodies and civil society; development of international
cooperation on sustainability issues.

Taking into account the content of the concept of national security, it is expedient to define the following as the main principles
of the organization and functioning of the national security system: comprehensiveness – taking coordinated measures against
any threats and crisis situations at all stages of the national security cycle; broad interaction – it assumes that all involved subjects
constantly exchange the necessary information, communicate
with each other in various formats, jointly perform certain tasks
within the limits of certain responsibilities; adaptability – the system's ability to adapt without significant loss of functionality to crisis conditions and new circumstances that have arisen under the
influence of a threat or crisis situation, to ensure survival, evolution, the ability to transform negative results into positive ones, as
well as to apply innovative solutions; predictability – timely identification of threats, detection of vulnerabilities and risk assessment;
reliability – assumes that the system functions fully and is able to
overcome work failures that arise under the influence of threats
and crisis situations, and all involved entities have sufficient and
developed capabilities to respond to threats and crisis situations;

awareness – assumes that all involved entities have the appropriate knowledge and practical skills to respond to threats and crisis situations at any stage; readiness – availability of action plans for joint response to any threats, appropriate level of theoretical and practical training of all involved subjects for response at all stages of the cycle of ensuring national stability; mobility – the ability to quickly attract main and reserve forces, means, resources and join efforts to solve tasks in the conditions of the realization of a threat, the onset of a crisis situation; redundancy – the presence of additional capacities in the system that can be used due to the fact that the main ones have failed, as well as alternative plans, development strategies; continuity – assumes that in a crisis situation or under the influence of a threat, the system continues to operate without a significant loss of functionality, and all involved entities are able to perform basic functions; and, finally, subsidiarity refers to a division of authority and responsibility whereby key decisions regarding response to threats and crisis situations are made at the lowest possible level with coordination at the highest appropriate level.

Conclusions to the first chapter

The formation of the direction of scientific research in the field of ensuring national stability took place as a result of the development and mutual enrichment of various scientific disciplines, primarily research of complex systems, sustainable development, and security research. It should be added that the development of science and technology, the emergence of new and strengthening of traditional threats have actualized the issue of the inadequacy of the national security system to new conditions and the search for new conceptual approaches and directions for its improvement. Despite the fact that the issue of building national stability is actively included in the agenda of many states and international organizations, it can be stated that at the moment a fixed definition of this concept, generally accepted criteria, methods of assessing national stability and requirements for building an appropriate system have not been adopted. Different interpretations of the concept of stability in the field of ensuring national security determine different approaches to the formation of state policy in the corresponding direction. Such an ambiguous situation makes it possible to change concepts, when, under the pretext of strengthening national stability, individual experts and officials propose multi-directional, unsystematic measures, the aggregate effectiveness of which will be insignificant, and the resource consumption will be high. Considering the fact that the modern security environment is becoming more aggressive toward the state and society, and the destructive effects on them are more destructive, the creation of an additional complex mechanism, the functioning of which is aimed at strengthening the stability of these system-forming objects, seems justified in the context of ensuring their security and further development in conditions of uncertainty. Such a complex mechanism is the system of ensuring national stability, the formation of which in practice should take into account fundamentally important theoretical conclusions and regularities within the concept of national stability. Among such conclusions, it is appropriate to single out, in particular, the fact that the state and society are complex systems, and their components may suffer from various threats to different degrees. In addition, passive security objects are able to transform into actors of their own resilience, and the growth of the total number of resilient objects and actors can strengthen national resilience in general.

CHAPTER 2

Methodological Toolkit
for Ensuring National Security

The development and implementation of any mechanisms and measures to ensure national security require the use of appropriate methodological tools, which make it possible to streamline relevant activities and determine priority goals and objectives. In the conditions when the development of national stability is a fairly new task for the state and society, the definition of conceptual approaches to the choice of a model of ensuring national security and the key parameters of the corresponding system, as well as the formation of an appropriate state policy taking into account the content and regularities of the concept of national security, is of particular importance.

2.1. Peculiarities of development and implementation of state policy in the sphere of ensuring national security

2.1.1. The role of the state in ensuring national security in the conditions of martial law

As already mentioned, the system of ensuring national security differs from the system of ensuring national security, in particular, by the principles of interaction of their subjects and the construction of systemic connections. It is important to find out how the role and functions of the state as one of the key actors differ in both cases. The discussion about the role of the state in the system of social relations is one of the main topics of political science. There has been a change in priorities: first of all, the security of people, not territories, investing in sustainable human development, not in weapons.

In the context of ensuring national security, this means the existence of a certain potential of potential and self-organization in the state and society, which can be directed in a given direction and strengthened thanks to state policy measures of the appropriate direction, which include, among other things, the development and complication of relations between various subjects and objects. Based on the conclusions of the above-mentioned research-

ers, the author can say that for the formation of a modern organizational model for ensuring national security and stability, it is
fundamentally important to find an optimal balance between the
processes of centralization and decentralization of state administration functions, as well as between state administration and
self-administration, also in the security sphere. The schematically
indicated processes are presented in Figure 2.1.

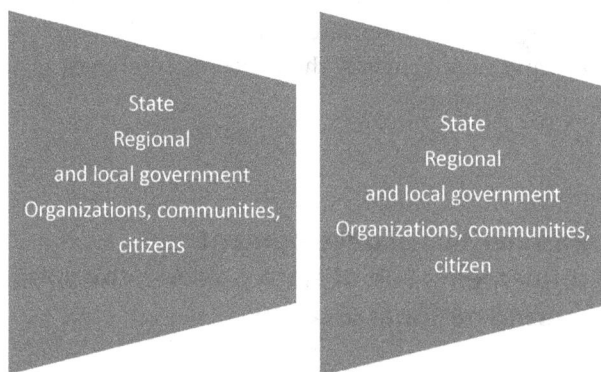

State
Regional
and local government
Organizations, communities,
citizens

State
Regional
and local government
Organizations, communities,
citizen

Figure 2.1. Balancing the principles of centralization and decentralization of
state power in the complex system of national security

Source: developed by the author.

A debate continues among modern researchers about how the
role of the state in ensuring national security should change in
modern conditions.

Therefore, there is a demand for the performance of new functions in the field of national security, which would correspond to
the essential characteristics of the concept of sustainability in the
field of national security. At the same time, it is also about a certain redistribution of powers, expansion of the role and scope of
responsibility of both the state and local authorities and the non-
state sector, including civil society, in countering a wide range of
threats. At the same time, one should also take into account the
specifics of self-organization and self-management as specific
manifestations of the formation of resilience. This question will be
analyzed more thoroughly later. Implementation of the concept
of national security in practice does not mean irresponsibility of
the state or a significant reduction in the scope of its powers in

the field of ensuring national security. First of all, it is about the redistribution of powers between the state and other subjects of ensuring national security.

This conclusion of an influential international organization became especially relevant for Ukraine with the beginning of the aggression of the Russian Federation, during which non-military measures aimed at the population of Ukraine (propaganda, spreading of disinformation, inciting inter-ethnic and inter-confessional enmity) became the main weapon of the aggressor. The synergistic effect of the interaction of the national security system security and the system of ensuring national stability is manifested primarily in the acquisition by objects and subjects of new properties that allow them to more effectively counteract threats and adapt to changes. And this requires improving the organization of their interaction. Taking into account the above, it can be concluded that the process of formation state policy in the field of ensuring national security and stability should acquire a comprehensive character. This is due to the fact that, on the one hand, such a policy should be aimed at ensuring the stability of the state itself, and on the other – at creating the necessary conditions for increasing the stability of other subjects, implementation of effective mechanisms for their cooperation. This requires finding the optimal balance between the respective goals under conditions of limited resources.

In the context of ensuring national stability, the state administration should primarily encourage various subjects to take actions aimed at strengthening their own capabilities, creating effective organizational formats for comprehensive interaction and proper motivation for such activities. The model of organizational support of national security can be based both on the distribution of responsibilities defined by legislation and on contractual principles. The latter is extremely important for establishing a public-private partnership, in particular determining the order of coordinated actions in crisis situations. It should be added that each of the subjects of ensuring national security should be aware not only of the long-term benefits of cooperation in this area, but also the amount of possible losses in the event of a crisis situation and the procedure for their full or partial compensation. At the same time, the coordinating and controlling functions of the state are strengthened. Such changes should be reflected in the formation and implementation of state policy in the sphere of ensuring national security.

2.1.2. Planning problems under martial law

In accordance with generally accepted norms and rules, the practical implementation of the goals and tasks of ensuring national security should take place on the basis of strategic and program documents of the state, primarily in the field of national security [11], it is especially difficult to plan in the conditions of a direct military conflict, as is the case with Ukraine in the conditions of a military state. However, planning in conditions of uncertainty is extremely complicated. In the long term, it becomes very difficult to determine specific target orientations, rather, only development vectors can be established. This actualizes the problem of improving the mechanisms of long-, medium-, and short-term planning, the solution of which requires proper scientific support. In particular, the development of methodological principles in the field of strategic planning and management, the study of world best practices and learning the lessons of one's own history help states to form security strategies that meet modern challenges and requirements [11]. H. Eisenkot and G. Shiboni note that ensuring national security depends on the existence of a national strategy that contains political, military, economic and behavioral sub-strategies, as well as those related to social, demographic and various other problems [20]. Classical approaches to strategic planning in the field of defense and corporate management are now actively used in the field of national security and do not lose their relevance. A feature of strategic planning in the field of national security is that the political, economic, informational, security and other capabilities created as a result, as well as forces and means, can be used both in peacetime and in wartime or in crisis situations to fulfill socially considered as an art and as a science of creating and using the political, economic and information capabilities of the state, as well as its armed forces in peacetime and wartime for the fulfillment of national tasks [13, p. 144]. Scientists pay attention to the importance of distinguishing between strategic planning and strategic management. At the same time, most scientists agree that the national security strategy is a state-wide non-detailed general plan of action, a set of rules for achieving long-term goals for ensuring the security and development of the state in accordance with defined national interests. A. Bucher, in addition, draws attention to the importance of security strategies for establishing integration and coordination of activities of various subjects of national security [64].

An important role in developing a national security strategy is played by the analysis of the security environment in order to identify current and future challenges and threats, as well as global, regional and national development trends. In modern conditions, strategic management in the field of national security is becoming increasingly important. J. Tama notes that the variability and unpredictability of the global security environment characteristic of the modern world increasingly complicates strategic planning in the field of national security and increases the requirements for organizing the relevant process. [35]. The development and implementation of a comprehensive state policy to ensure national security and stability, on the one hand, provides the state's security policy with greater flexibility and adaptability to rapid changes in the security environment, and on the other hand, responding to a wide range of threats, including hybrids, the state and society provide appropriate training. The creation of national security strategies on this basis, for example, has been carried out for a long time in Great Britain and the Netherlands. As noted above, the classical system of ensuring national security is gradually losing its effectiveness in conditions of significant changes in the global security environment. Since it cannot guarantee complete protection against all threats, it demonstrates incomplete compatibility with predetermined goals. In addition, threats, especially hybrid ones, are becoming increasingly difficult to predict. Although some mechanisms for ensuring national security remain sufficiently reliable, the question arose of supplementing them with other mechanisms that show greater effectiveness in conditions of uncertainty. This indicates the need to improve the system for ensuring national security by combining it with the system for ensuring national stability. The corresponding changes should be reflected in the strategic and program documents of the state.

Based on the essential characteristics of the concept of national security formulated in the first section of the monograph, it is possible to identify a set of new tasks, the solution of which, among other issues, strategic and program documents should be aimed at state from the point of view of national security in modern conditions. Among these tasks: implementation of a comprehensive approach against a wide range of threats at different stages; adjustment effect.

2.2. Formation of a model of ensuring national security based on a systemic approach

2.2.1. Peculiarities of choosing the key parameters of the national security model under martial law

One of the key issues in the formation of state policy in the field of national security is the choice of a model that determines the specifics of the organization of the system of ensuring national stability, which best meets the needs of a specific state and its society. This presupposes, first of all, the determination of goals, priorities, features of the organization of system connections, a specific set of mechanisms for ensuring national stability – key parameters for the organization of the system for ensuring national stability.

Analytics of a specific military security model allows us to determine how effectively and quickly the system responds to signals from the security environment in the form of dangerous trends, processes, phenomena, ultimately, threats and crisis situations. The results obtained during the analysis show whether the selected model is compatible with the effectiveness goals. Various models of the national security system are united by a common goal – to reduce the level of dangerous consequences of the implementation of threats and ensure the continuous functioning of the main spheres of life of society and the state before and after the crisis, including adaptation to the consequences of threats and rapid changes in the security environment.

Given the limited resources of the state and society, it is impossible to achieve all these goals simultaneously. The central argument in most scientific and political debates is that most modern threats are inevitable, unpredictable or difficult to predict. This determines the main focus of the national stability model in favor of reactive rather than preventive measures, reducing the impact of threats and ensuring the continuity of social development, rather than mechanisms that provide the possibility of rapid recovery after a crisis.

At the practical level, one can observe the application in different countries of a broad or narrow approach to the organization of the national stability system within the framework of the chosen model. Within the framework of the broad approach, the principles of stability are applied in all areas of national security and public administration, including economic, social, environmental, foreign policy, etc., as well as in public relations.

The narrow approach to ensuring national security assumes that the basis is primarily the improvement of anti-crisis management in the field of protecting the population and critical state facilities from various threats and dangers (primarily natural, artificial, biological, terrorist or military in nature), as well as ensuring the continuity of the implementation of the most important functions of the state (especially management, supply of energy, water and food, transport and communications, provision of primary medical care, the ability to cope with mass displacement of people, significant human losses or the spread of dangerous diseases, etc.). At the same time, the system of protection of the population from emergencies and the system of protection of critical infrastructure facilities are generally key universal mechanisms for ensuring stability. The principles of stability are most fully applied in crisis management systems, in particular in countries such as Norway, Denmark, Sweden, Great Britain and the United States.

Martial law is a special legal regime that is introduced in the event of aggression by a foreign state or an immediate threat of aggression. Based on this definition, the author can conclude that a state of emergency can be introduced in the presence of a threat to the external component of sovereignty (aggression, threat of aggression); in all other circumstances of an extraordinary nature (including internal threats to the security of the state, to people's lives) a state of emergency is introduced. All these regimes are accompanied by a restriction for a certain period of time of the constitutional rights and freedoms of man and citizen.

The martial law regime is regulated within the framework of the constitutional legislation of foreign countries and Ukraine with a greater or lesser degree of detail. As a rule, within the borders of the states of the European Union, the regime of martial law is reflected in detail (due to the introduction of restrictions on human rights within the framework of the introduction of this regime). Often, issues of martial law are regulated directly by the basic law of the state.

In the United States of America, there is no clear distinction between a state of war and a state of emergency (the former takes precedence). In general, it can be noted that the declaration of war (introduction of martial law) belongs to the competence of Congress. The introduction of a state of emergency both on a separate territory and on the entire territory of the state is carried out by the president by adopting an act in the form of a resolution, which is immediately sent to Congress and published in the official publication "Federal Register." However, both states of emergency and martial law are terminated by a corresponding resolution of the Houses of Congress, by an act of the president or by the end of the term of its introduction.

In the event that a foreign state or other subjects of international relations commit armed actions, the object of which is security, territorial integrity, the foundations of the constitutional order, which create a significant threat to the normal life of people, property, a state of emergency, or a state of emergency may be introduced. Police forces are used to stop the listed military operations. Only if the required results cannot be achieved, the defense forces are used. If the parliament cannot take these decisions due to lack of time, circumstances that make it impossible for the parliament to sit, a state of political crisis may arise. In case of declaration of a political crisis, the decision to introduce one of the above-mentioned regimes is taken by the president independently by means of a decree, which is valid for 30 days, after which it needs the approval of the Parliament.

2.2.2. Methodological principles of creating mechanisms of adaptive management of national security in conditions of martial law

An important goal of adaptive national security management is to maintain the processes and main indicators of the functioning of the state and society within the framework of dynamic equilibrium. In the first section of the monograph, it was noted that the choice of the optimal level of national security in general and its individual components (levels of specific stability) in particular is important for the formation of state policy in the appropriate direction, since it establishes clear guidelines. It should be remembered that the definition of appropriate target guidelines without taking into account the context of the situation and time frames can significantly deform state policy and disorient the subjects of ensuring national security and stability. Therefore, the optimal level of national security and other target guidelines are variables that must be periodically reviewed and clarified on the basis of adaptive management. Ensuring national security combines different spheres and systems (economic, environmental, social, organizational, military, law enforcement, etc.): all of them must meet the main criteria for sustainability. At the same time, the definition of target guidelines for different spheres of activity must take into account their specifics. When planning and implementing measures to ensure national security, resources must be considered as limiting factors. The allocation of resources requires finding compromise solutions and balancing different interests not only within the framework of state policy in the field of national security and stability, but also between politicians of states of different orientations. World experience shows that many countries now practice an integrated approach to ensuring readiness and effectiveness of response to a wide range of threats and rapid recovery after a crisis, according to which issues of civil protection of the population and crisis management are considered together with other aspects of ensuring national security and defense. Excessive concentration of power in one center increases the risk of cessation of the performance of functions critical to society in the event of the collapse of state administration. In this regard, it is necessary to transfer a reasonable amount of authority and resources to the places, which also involves the creation or strengthening of local security and defense forces, in particular units of territorial defense, civil defense, public order, the involvement of citizens' associations. in active cooperation, the development of partnerships between the state and the private sector in the field of security, etc.

Examples of successful functioning of security forces and territorial defense are the National Guard and decentralized police service in the United States, the functioning of local police support forces in England and local fire brigades in most Western countries. Also widespread is the practice of involving public associations in cooperation with authorized state institutions on certain issues that ensure national stability, public-private partnerships in the field of national security are developing. In general, the reform of the security and defense sector, which reflects the continuous process of development of relevant state bodies and their management systems, as well as their adaptation to the conditions of new security, should be carried out in modern conditions, taking into account the principles of ensuring stability. In the context of the formation of mechanisms for adaptive management of national security, the creation and implementation of a system for early detection and prevention of threats, especially in the context of the spread of hybrid threats [105]. Such threats, as a rule, are hidden in nature or are implemented through the manipulation of democratic values and legal mechanisms, they are very difficult to identify at the initial stage and predict their development, since they are nonlinear in nature.

An effective tool for identifying relevant vulnerabilities ("weak links" in the security and defense sector) can be a comprehensive review of the security and defense sector, as well as a review of the stability of state authorities and local governments. An effective tool in the early detection of threats and the definition of operational response measures are situation centers, which can be formed in state authorities. Joining efforts by creating a network of situation centers makes it possible to implement the principles of broad interaction and a comprehensive approach to threat analysis.

To implement these tasks, the situational center must ensure the following key functions: gathering information about a certain field of activity; definition of criteria for its evaluation; data processing for the purpose of identifying influencing factors; construction of analysis models; design of management decisions and their implementation; monitoring and evaluation of the results of decision implementation. In the context of ensuring national stability, the formation of a network of situational centers is an important, but not the only element in the system of early detection and prevention of threats. The principle of broad interaction involves the active involvement of civil society at all stages of the cycle of ensuring national stability, as well as the creation of permanent bilateral communication channels. In this context, the experience of various countries deserves attention: Great Britain – regarding the functioning of the network of local sustainability forums and the formation of the National Register of Threats; the USA and Israel – regarding the involvement of the population in providing support to law enforcement agencies in countering terrorist activity and building public resistance to this threat; Estonia – regarding the role of civil society in identifying and countering threats in the information and cyber spheres, etc. The OSCE Bureau for Democratic Institutions and Human Rights, together with the Department for Countering Transnational Threats of the OSCE Secretariat, prepared a guidance report "Preventing terrorism and countering violent extremism and radicalization leading to terrorism: an approach based on police-community interaction," which addressed in particular, issues related to the involvement of specific categories of the population of organizations, ethnic minorities, and representatives of small and medium-sized businesses in the relevant activities [27].

Effective interaction of state bodies and civil society in the context of ensuring national stability, including at the stage of early warning of threats to national security, requires proper organization and coordination of such activities. In world practice, this function is mainly performed by an executive body or a specially formed service within it. So, in Great Britain it is the Cabinet Office, in the USA it is the Federal Emergency Management Agency within the Ministry of Homeland Security (Department of Homeland Security (DHS) Federal Emergency Management Agency (FEMA)). Separately, it should be emphasized the importance of the timely implementation of a set of measures to ensure cyber security and information protection in authorized state authorities, in particular in the network of situational centers, as well as the formation of a high-quality personnel reserve in the field of ensuring national security and stability.

2.3. Assessment of risks and capabilities, identification of threats and vulnerabilities in the field of national security as martial law

2.3.1. The expediency of creating a national risk assessment system under martial law conditions

As noted, uncertainty and variability are characteristics of the modern world. J. Fixel argues that predictability has become an anachronism and decision-making must take place in the context of a wide range of changing possibilities. This raises doubts about the reliability of forecasts developed in the security sector, especially for the long term, and the possibility of using such information in the formation of relevant state policy [22]. Under such conditions, the assessment process as a component of national security management requires certain clarifications. Determining the future (primarily likely threats and emergencies) is of less value than finding solutions that ensure the flexibility of security policy and the readiness of subjects to respond to unforeseen crisis situations. As has been proven, in the context of ensuring national stability, it is more expedient to use an adaptive management model, an important component of which, according to K. Holling, is assessment. It should be carried out on an ongoing basis, as it provides the necessary information for choosing and clarifying ways of further development and policy adjustment [25]. As noted in the first section of the monograph, the state and functionality of the system and its individual elements can be assessed for compliance with the criteria of stability. At the same time, in the context of ensuring national security and stability, risk assessment is no less important. The author are talking about the influences of the external and internal security environment. Risk assessment allows you to timely identify both dangerous and promising trends in the development of the state and society, identify threats, identify vulnerabilities, which, ultimately, contributes to the formation of state strategic documents and action plans in the event of crisis situations., allows you to timely correct them, etc. Due to the fact that risks to the state and society can arise in different areas and have different consequences, their analysis should be carried out comprehensively, on a systematic basis. It should be noted that in the scientific and professional literature there are different definitions of the concepts of "risk," "threat," "challenge," "danger," "vulnerability," as well as different research approaches to determining the relationships between them. observed. These words are often used synonymously.

It is worth emphasizing that risk is only a possibility, not a guarantee of an undesirable outcome caused by certain events, activities, etc. At the same time, threats are directly related to certain events, activities or inaction of people, organizations, states that can or intend to cause harm/damage to others. Currently, there are methods for assessing both risks and threats. The study "National Risk and Threat Assessment Systems: Best World Practice, New Opportunities for Ukraine" [12] determined that the effective functioning of the risk assessment system is an element of the importance of early detection and prevention of threats, strategic planning and ensuring national security and stability. Such systems are called national because they operate at the state level, include processes related to ensuring the security of the state, society and each citizen, and are also based on broad interaction and cooperation between departments. The use of modern methods and technologies for risk assessment and threat identification, crisis modeling, and scenario forecast development all help to increase the reliability of the results obtained, as well as to form a broad evidence base for further analysis. In conditions of rapid and unpredictable changes in the security environment, the overall picture of threats is of much less value than the typologies, multi-criteria matrixes, model catalogs, and scenario forecasts developed on its basis. They are necessary for further definition of protocols for coordinated actions to respond to threats of various natures and origins, as well as for planning appropriate measures. National risk assessment systems operate in many countries of the world. As world experience shows, despite certain differences in the organization of such systems, they all have a number of common features, for example, their purpose and the main areas of use of the results obtained (Table 2.1).

Table 2.1 Common features of national risk assessment systems Characteristics Manifestations Purpose of the system

Manifestation	Characteristics
Appointment systems	• Assessment and ranking of all possible risks for the state and society; • identification of dangerous trends and threats to the national security; • search for new opportunities for the development of the state and society; • identification of vulnerabilities in the state and society; • formation of databases on risks, threats and their consequences; • provision of exchange of information on risks for of national security
Directions using results assessment	• Adjustment of state policy in the field of provision national security and stability; • development of projects of strategic and program documents states; • development of mechanisms and individual measures in the field of provision national security and stability; • formation of plans and protocols of coordinated actions in case responding to threats or crisis situations of any kind origins at various stages of their deployment; • informing the population about current and predicted threats and crisis situations

The main essence of the functioning of the national risk assessment system is to establish typical groups of risks and their consequences for specific target groups, assess the probability of their implementation and the possible scale and severity of their consequences. Based on the results of the analysis of relevant information, universal protocols for coordinated actions to respond to major threats and crisis situations at different stages of their deployment should be developed, as well as specific methods by which risks can be assessed in different areas. However, the development and implementation of a unified methodology for assessing risks and their consequences, as well as identifying threats to national security are extremely important, as they will allow their end-to-end comparison and classification in different areas based on a single principle and criteria. National risk assessment systems also allow for the identification of dangerous trends and threats to national security, vulnerabilities in the state and society. The information obtained is used by the state leadership and authorized state bodies to make decisions on the formation and implementation of relevant state policy, planning measures to increase the level of readiness of the state and society to a wide range of threats, and developing the necessary capabilities, as well as the distribution of public financial resources. In developed countries, the national risk assessment system is an element of strategic planning in the field of national security (Figure 2.2).

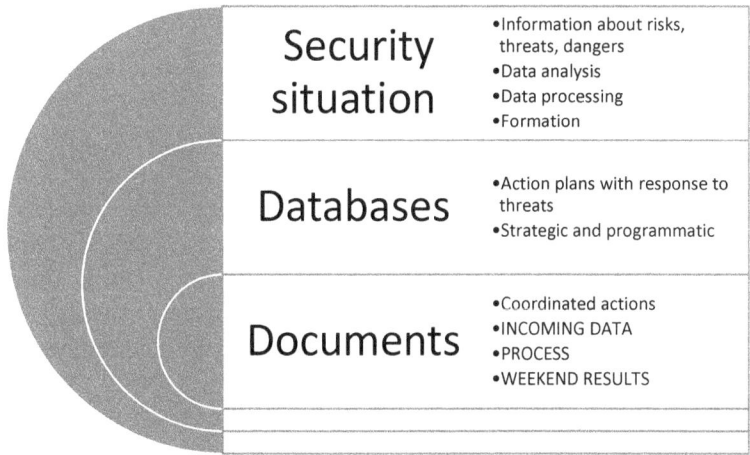

Figure 2.2. General scheme of functioning of the national risk assessment system

Source: compiled by the author.

According to the results of the study of the features of the functioning of national risk assessment systems in different countries, it can be concluded that in general, such systems are aimed not only at identifying risks and threats to the state and society, but also cover a larger number of processes related to ensuring national security and stability and form an algorithm for a comprehensive assessment of risks and opportunities, identifying threats and identifying vulnerabilities.

2.3.2. Algorithm of complex assessment of risks and capabilities, identification of threats and detection of vulnerabilities in conditions of martial law

The risk assessment methodology may differ in different countries. According to the results of familiarization with the recommendations of organizations aimed at the selection of stages. The principle of a comprehensive assessment of the scope [12].

Stage 1. Analysis of the security situation.

At this stage:

- determination of the general context of the situation;
- key communities of the national security state in different meanings with their critical values;
- determination of trends and new directions of development of the state and society in the long term.

Stage 2. Determination of the greatest national security, determination of protection (screening):

1) All assessments in accordance with the probability and seriousness of the needs of companies. The Delphi method can usually be done in this way. any expert knowledge, shortcomings of this safe method of assessments, different professional level of experts, the possibility of manipulation by those who generalize the results, etc.;

2) First, the implementation of the security environment is carried out in the context of certain areas (for example, society, sociopolitical, etc.). At different times, countries define such national security as one in which control and constant commitment are required. The security environment in experts for checks determined on control, as well as reducing the list for a larger number of security requests on the probability and seriousness of companies. At the same time, the level of concern may be lower, since for the latter, in addition to expert assessments, there is also statistical statistics. Various logarithmic scales and research methods for assessing the available reserve. This is

an opportunity to determine the most correct information and have the probability of occurrence and the most acquired. In addition, for the further development of scenario reviews, the list of solutions can be supplemented in such a way that the greatest impact is knocked down, as well as those that have a probability but a small impact. V. Smil in the study "Disasters and Global Trends: 50s" described the organization of global ones by the degree of probability of their occurrence. Therefore, the scientist distinguishes the main groups of knowledge:

a) disasters, the probability of which can be estimated due to their periodic nature;
b) possible disasters that have not occurred before;
c) theoretical disasters, the probability of which can only be calculated theoretically.

The forecast estimates of this science are responsible for the degree of probability of the occurrence of a particular phenomenon or process in 50 or 100 years, as well as the scale of company activities [13]. The methodology used by experts of the World Economic Forum to assess the global [109] is to use various research methods, including questionnaires, introduction, generalization, extrapolation, systematization and formation. At the same time, the proposed methodology is not very verifiable, as evidenced by a comparison of the predicted with the actual results that they have based on the results of previous years. In addition, this methodology has the ability to identify the connections and influence between different global funds, as well as the consequences of new rights, and the consequences of these products can be observed as a result of various studies for assessment and forecasting. When solving the problem, it is advisable to involve experts in the risk assessment process and develop studies of the security environment.

Stage 3. In-depth analysis of companies, development of scenario forecasts, modeling the existence of the territory. Any risk can be possible, such as one: affecting the lives of people, society and the state, both typical for a group of companies and atypical, or an escape of opportunities, that is, a node that can give a certain potential for development. The set of risks and their consequences in a multidimensional matrix that has been used for more analysis. The cumulative scale of possible consequences of each risk should be assessed according to the criteria of severity, number, duration, etc. A thorough analysis of such consequences can change the priority of the greatest threats identified. Taking into account world experience, it is recommended to determine the consequences of exposure to risks and threats in relation to the following basic groups of objects: physical objects (residential, administrative buildings, networks, etc.); human capital (life, health, well-being of the population); economic and financial resources; environment (natural resources, ecological situation, etc.); social and political capital (formal and informal social ties and networks, governance systems, political institutions, peace and security, etc.). Depending on the needs of the industry or the sphere of social relations, special target groups can be selected (for example, children, people of working age, pensioners, etc.). It is recommended to identify target groups that may be most negatively affected by the threat, as well as those that have sufficient resilience potential and are able to independently combat the threat with an acceptable loss of functionality. In order to assess the consequences of the manifestation of threats, indicators such as the possibility of losing territory, the deployment of destructive processes in society, the destruction of critical infrastructure objects, economic losses, etc. should be used for the purposes of relevant protection. The criteria for analyzing risks and threats according to the consequences may vary in different countries. Thus, in the United States, the main objects of possible impact of risks and threats are recognized as the state and the population in general, as well as areas of critical importance, in particular social relations, economy, ecology, public administration. To assess risks and identify threats in a certain industry (area of responsibility), it is recommended to use the following main groups of indicators: indicators of the state of security of the industry; the probability of the threat being realized; the scale of possible consequences. Taking into account the data received, scenario forecasts are developed, simulating crisis situations. Using comparative analysis methods, scenario forecasts can be classified using various criteria and assumptions. After classification, priority scenario forecasts are considered in three variants: optimistic, pessimistic and realistic, taking into account the defined threshold of acceptable risk.

Stage 4. Assessment of capabilities. In some countries, the risk assessment is completed after the above stages and does not take into account the state of the capabilities necessary to overcome current and prospective threats to national security. However, this stage is extremely important in the context of further planning of measures to respond to threats and crisis situations and increasing the level of preparedness of the state and society for such a response. Comparing the state of capabilities with risk and threat assessments makes it possible to identify the vulnerabilities of the state, society, as well as the system of ensuring national security and stability, and to take timely measures to eliminate them. Therefore, when assessing capabilities, it is advisable to determine the ability of state institutions, systems, and institutions to effectively respond to the development of a crisis situation (the realization of a threat) in relation to the following stages of the cycle of ensuring national stability:

1) ensuring readiness for response. At this stage of the cycle of ensuring national stability, it is recommended to use the following main criteria for assessment: reliability (availability of the necessary resources, regulation of legal and organizational aspects of activity, dissemination of necessary knowledge and skills among response subjects, conducting training, taking measures to prevent the threat, etc.); redundancy (availability of reserves in all types of resources, taking into account the specifics of the industry and reservation standards); adaptability (availability of alternative sources of supply of critical state functions and development strategies, response plans for forecasts of various scenarios, as well as flexibility and efficiency of management systems); absorption (ability to accept and accommodate a significant number of victims, forced migrants, refugees, provide necessary social support, etc.); and 2) responsiveness.

Stage 6. Complex mapping, geospatial support (eng. geospatial support) Geospatial data analysis is a modern, high-tech method for assessing the situation of security and detect threats. It makes it possible to combine the databases available in the state (meteorological, geological, infrastructural, medical, etc.) into a single geographic information system that operates in real time and allows for forecasting based on the results of constant monitoring. The general operational picture is established thanks to the collection of information, its sorting, generalization, processing using analytical and technical means. Information on the development of the situation is provided to the authorized structures that concern them. Filling such an information system with data can be carried out, in particular, with the help of a network of situational centers. They can have permanent access to the results of information processing by the system. The advantage of the specified information system is that it allows the analysis of many risks in space and time, taking into account their mutual influences, and comparing them with existing capabilities. This increases the efficiency of interdepartmental cooperation, eliminates duplication of work, and creates conditions for making decisions based on real data.

Stage 7. Dissemination of risk assessment results, visualization. Often, a comprehensive report on identified threats, possible scenarios for the development of crisis situations and their consequences (or most of them) is recognized as confidential and not subject to publication. Usually, the lead organization also maintains a public risk register. It explains to citizens in a simple and easy way what dangers they may encounter in everyday life, what these dangers and their consequences can manifest, how to respond to them correctly, and which authorized bodies to contact. These national registers of risks and threats can be found in public access, in particular on the official websites of the governments of Great Britain, New Zealand, the Netherlands and other countries. This makes it possible to increase the level of public awareness of the nature and manifestations of the main threats and dangers, as well as the degree of readiness of society for the necessary response.

Stage 8. Monitoring and reassessing risks based on lessons learned According to the principles of adaptive management, the results of the risk and capability assessment, threat identification and vulnerability discovery should be reviewed and updated periodically.

2.3.3. Basic research methods used for risk assessment

Many studies have been devoted to the methodology of evaluating processes and results in complex systems, among which it is worth highlighting works. According to the conclusions of these authors, it is possible to characterize the main assumptions on the basis of which appropriate evaluations should be carried out: any result that can be detected is subject to evaluation (quantitative or qualitative); the determination of the results to be evaluated cannot be separated from the determination of the properties (characteristics) that form the results; the validity of data for assessment involves their reliability and compliance with the defined goals. The main problematic issues of evaluation, according to Ch. Churchman's definition, are the following: language – how to formulate the results of calculations in such a way as to convey them to others without distorting the content; detailing – what data and how much of it should be used for calculations depending on the defined task; standardization – definition of conditions, compliance with which will guarantee correctness and objectivity of calculations; and accuracy and control – the need to evaluate deviations and control the results in different conditions [15].

Despite the fact that integrated risk assessment has a complex interdisciplinary nature, the most common research methods currently used in national risk assessment systems can be distinguished. Statistical modeling of the environment, which allows analyzing (in the historical dimension of time) the relationships between the frequency of crisis situations, primarily natural disasters, changes in characteristics and their consequences using: the observation method; using the extrapolation method to predict the possible nature of the occurrence of risks based on the identified trends and analysis of threshold values, as well as providing an assessment of economic and other losses. Within the framework of statistical modeling of the environment, studies are conducted of the characteristics of past crisis situations that have the property of cyclical recurrence, their comparison with the characteristics of the development of the modern security environment; modeling of combinations of risk manifestations. Based on the corresponding analysis, a quantitative assessment of the predicted consequences of crisis situations in the event of their recurrence (financial losses, scale of infrastructure destruction, human losses, etc.) is formed. The calculations use official statistical information and the results of thematic analytical studies. Software modeling of the consequences of crisis situations. Thanks to computer modeling of disasters, a large number of "hypothetical" crisis situations are modeled, based on the regularity of the random and unpredictable nature of their occurrence. Digital catalogs of simulated disasters are formed, which contain a description of the scenarios for the development of emergency situations and other crisis situations and numerical indicators of their consequences. A number of priority risk scenarios are developed. This methodological approach is based on probability theory and mathematical statistics. Risk assessment through consultations and decision-making by a wide range of experts in the format of thematic meetings, interdepartmental forums, scientific conferences, etc.

The most common are the Delphi technique and the Cooke method. Both methods involve creating a group of professional experts and giving each of them the opportunity to independently assess the probability and consequences of risks, as well as to determine the range of uncertainty of their manifestation. In the future, the materials of the group of experts will be analyzed and the weighted average indicator of risk assessment will be derived. To assess the probability and consequences of crisis situations, the method of objective calibration is used, according to which each expert determines the upper, middle and lower limit values of the probability and consequences of risks in accordance with the developed parameters. The application of correction coefficients for the quality of experts involved in this type of assessment makes it possible to reduce the level of subjectivity and increase the level of reliability of assessments and forecasts. Features of determining the accuracy and reliability of experts' forecasts are described, in particular [6]. In general, as evidenced by world experience, various combinations of the above-mentioned main research methods are used in national risk assessment systems.

2.3.4. Formation of passports and threat registers

Passports and threat registers are a convenient form of systematization of the results of strategic analysis, which are used for planning and adaptive management in the field of national security. Their formation facilitates the implementation of constant monitoring of the situation in the spheres of national security, contributes to the timely adjustment of state policy in the relevant direction and its individual measures. As determined by Ukrainian scientists H. Sytnyk, V. Abramov, V. Mandragelya, "a threat passport (matrix) is a document that provides for the identification (assessment) of events, phenomena, processes, and other factors that create a danger of the realization of vital national interests of Ukraine, the characteristics of their possible development, as well as the definition of the main organizational, legal and other mechanisms regarding the activity of subjects of national security in response to threats" [13, c. 27–28]. V. Bogdanovych, A. Semenchenko, and M. Yezheev also emphasized the expediency of developing such documents and creating relevant databases [3]. Taking into account the results of the analysis of relevant scientific literature, it is possible to propose forming a passport of the threat from three main parts: the first contains the characteristics of the threat; the second defines the capabilities necessary to respond to the threat; the third contains universal protocols of coordinated actions to respond to a threat [108]. The description of the threat presented in the first part of the passport makes it possible to identify certain events and/or phenomena as a threat according to the established criteria; determine the factors that form it; factors (events, phenomena, processes) contributing to the realization of the threat; possible consequences for national security, target groups, etc. The second part of the threat passport defines the organizational and legal mechanisms and resources of the authorized state bodies, necessary for effective response to the threat in relation to the stages of the cycle of ensuring national stability. For the formation of the first two parts of the threat passport, it is advisable to use the results of a comprehensive assessment of risks, their consequences, as well as a review of capabilities, which was discussed in the monograph above.

Analysis of the security situation and the state of capabilities, carried out on the basis of threat passports, allows national security and stability entities to identify dangerous trends and factors of influence that require increased attention and immediate response, as well as the strengths and weaknesses of their activities and interaction with other secondary objects, and to adjust action plans in a timely manner. Currently, the practice of forming a national threat register has become widespread in the world; it is used, in particular, in the United Kingdom, the Netherlands,

New Zealand and other countries. In expanded form, such registers contain generalized results of a comprehensive assessment of risks and capabilities, identification of threats and vulnerabilities, as well as conclusions and recommendations for the formation of state policy, including in the field of ensuring national security and stability, which are not subject to publication. They are also an important tool for planning security and resilience measures at all levels (national, regional, local). In a public abbreviated form, such registers are an important tool for disseminating knowledge about the security situation, current threats and mechanisms for responding to them, primarily from the point of view of the interaction of the population with the authorized bodies of state power and local self-government. Taking into account the results of the analysis of world experience, it can be said that the relevant document can consist of three main parts:

1) a general description of the current security situation and trends in its development, as well as threats to national security and the consequences of their implementation that require the greatest attention;

2) a generalized description of each of the priority threats and crisis situations, which includes: a description of their manifestations and possible consequences, determination of the scope of responsibility and the procedure for responding to authorized bodies of state power and local self-government; informing the population about the procedure for maximum ensuring the safety of themselves, their families, property, etc.; necessary contact numbers of authorized bodies of state power and local self-government, links to useful electronic resources;

3) a description of the methodology for compiling the register. It should be noted that in the countries whose experience was studied, an authorized state body or institution responsible for the preparation, maintenance, publication and periodic updating of the national threat register has been identified. The public register is placed on the official website of such a state body/institution or on a separate page of the state information portal. Regional threat registers can be compiled on the basis of the national register, taking into account both the national situation and regional characteristics. Therefore, the formation of national and regional threat registers contributes to increasing the level of prepared-

ness of various entities for possible threats and large-scale crisis situations, the formation of unified approaches to identifying threats, increasing the effectiveness of interagency cooperation on the ground. national security, etc.

2.3.5. Organizational support of the national risk assessment system

The effectiveness of the functioning of the national risk assessment system depends on its proper legal and organizational support. The main principle of organizing such a system is broad interagency interaction. The corresponding systems can be created and operate both at the national and at the regional and local levels. National legislation generally determines the state body or institution responsible for coordinating activities in the field of risk and threat assessment and maintaining the national risk register, as well as the powers, duties and accountability of state and local government bodies, institutions and organizations participating in this process.

A general description of the organization of the national risk assessment system is presented in Figure 2.4.

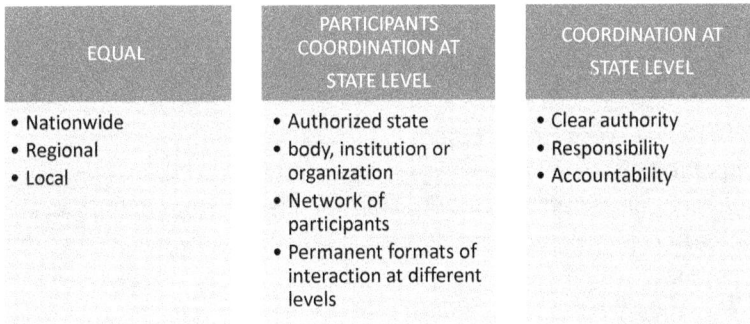

EQUAL	PARTICIPANTS COORDINATION AT STATE LEVEL	COORDINATION AT STATE LEVEL
• Nationwide • Regional • Local	• Authorized state • body, institution or organization • Network of participants • Permanent formats of interaction at different levels	• Clear authority • Responsibility • Accountability

Figure 2.4. Peculiarities of the organization of the national risk assessment system

Source: added by author.

An informal approach to fraud at the state level can also be observed. For example, in Switzerland, the provision of sector- and region-specific information to the central government for planning and implementation is a voluntary, decentralized responsibility. Such measures can only be effective if such assistance is part of national policies to ensure national security and stability, and create the necessary conditions for assistance in the country. An effective national risk assessment is most likely to occur in the early stages of a national crisis, when special circumstances and political and cultural processes are renewed. Currently, in many countries, governments have invested resources to reduce national conflicts and disasters, and to reap economic benefits. The basis for such reviews is carried out by a cross-functional working group, comprising representatives of ministries and agencies. Scientific institutions and independent experts can join the project. Therefore, a network of analysts has been established in the Netherlands to assess risks, comprising government research institutions, academic institutions and private organizations. In Great Britain, such approaches are associated with natural disaster prevention measures. As international experience has demonstrated, the multiple dimensions of risk and conflict resolution are particularly relevant when the impacts of violence are concentrated at the national, regional and/or local levels. Such a situation is also reflected in the development and implementation of best practices in the regional regions and in the areas of regional drought control. Networks of local and state officials for moderate risk and risk management have been built at the local level, including communities, communities, urban agencies and institutions, among others. Such networks of regions establish registries of physicians, based on regional recommendations, to establish a registry of physician-reported physicians. Specifically, in Great Britain, there is a group for local development (association for local development); in the Kingdom of the Netherlands security districts are involved in this process.

Among the key factors for multinational climate change, OECD experts have identified the following: a lack of skilled trade; reducing the cost of production, which is the reduction in the cost of production of certain assets; accessibility and accessibility; challenges in measuring national energy resources and managing transitions; cultural abundance; there is no political will in the state to implement such policies, and so on [19]. A comprehensive threat assessment program is an essential part of the strategy for ensuring national security and stability. This underscores the importance of social protection programs in times of uncertainty and uncertainty in the national economy. At the same time, the perception of inaccurate, misleading or hypocritical narratives, especially in terms of national stereotypes, racial and ethnic stereotypes (target groups included), as well as inconsistencies in judging outcomes, bad feelings or uncertainty about the political process. If we consider governance reforms as political, then, as a consequence, actions based on the negative consequences of problem analysis (along with the priorities and strategies to solve them), are the worst ones in such a situation are possible than "improved" [5].

Conclusions to the second chapter

The implementation of the concept of national stability involves clarifying the theoretical and practical consequences of the formation of state policy within the framework of national security. First of all, it is about the redistribution of the role and power of the state in the direction of ensuring national security and stability. In the context of building an effective systemic connection, it is important to achieve an appropriate balance between centralization and decentralization of public health activities in areas of interest. It should be noted that in developing countries, especially in developing ones, and in a period when the social infrastructure has not yet been formed, the infrastructure plays an important role in ensuring national stability. However, the role of other actors in maintaining national stability increases over time. They become responsible not only for individual tasks assigned to them, but also for many tasks. Given that the basic social structures (society, class society, institutions and establishments, enterprises, citizenship) contribute to self-determination and self-determination, such a work ethic is key in the state. The legal framework of subsidiarity, which is a key factor in ensuring national stability, ensures an effective first-line response to threatening and crisis situations, which builds or strengthens local security potential, social capital, etc., accordingly requires ensuring national stability with the maximum influence of local governments and regional groups. At the same time, it plays a key role in addressing strategic issues in ensuring national security and stability, in strengthening its rules and institutions. Promoting the redistribution of responsibilities within the framework of ensuring national stability can contribute to increasing the level of readiness of states and communities, as well as regional and local communities to respond to a wide range of threats, including hybrid ones.

CHAPTER 3

Foreign Experience of Martial State
in the Security Sphere

3.1. Changes in the strategic and program documents of the EU regarding the conditions of martial law of the Union and member states

The issue of ensuring national stability has acquired new significance for most European countries, as well as for international organizations, with the emergence of new challenges and challenges, including hybrid ones, especially in the context of the broader political transition after 2014, and has shown that the weakness of the institutions (formerly the UN, OSCE) that contributed to peace and stability after World War II. The issue of ensuring national stability has gained even greater attention in the context of the COVID-19 pandemic. Radical changes in the global security landscape have forced individual states and international organizations to reconsider ideological approaches to ensuring the stability of states and societies for the new reality. Leading countries and international organizations in the world now feel the need to develop and implement new and existing mechanisms for ensuring national stability. At the same time, in recent years, a large number of works by various academic and international organizations, as well as recommendations by individual experts, have appeared in the titles of which the word "resilience" is used. This raises the question of the need to test them against national standards.

In the context of the EU gender equality framework, there is growing interest in ensuring the quality and effectiveness of health systems [12]. This is due to the fact that most emergencies (especially natural disasters) cannot be completely avoided, while minimizing their negative consequences for society and the state. Given that the initial response to disasters and catastrophes must take place directly where they occur, ensuring the capacity of personnel ready to respond to disasters and catastrophes at regional and local levels is paramount. Local and regional authorities play an important role in EU member states. Multi-employer mechanisms for ensuring stability and responding to threats should be regulated not only by national legislation, but also by EU law, as well as international law. In particular, the Sendai Regional Strategy for a Climate Change Mitigation Framework 2015–2030 should take into account the interrelationships in this region [93]. The European Union played a leading role in its final negotiations and supported all countries (excluding EU members and member states) in achieving their goals. In June 2016, the European Commission launched the Sendai Regional Strategy (2016) on climate change emergency activities. The tools developed are used in EU countries at all levels and include, in particular: collection and compilation of data on loss and damage from emergency response, assessment of experience, risk assessment, policy issues in terms of effectiveness, ensuring adequate infrastructure in cities, risk reduction and risk-based empowerment. In many EU countries, local and regional authorities take legal and policy decisions. They are often the frontline government institutions in mitigating the effects of natural disasters. At EU level, the implementation of the Sendai Framework will be supported by local and regional authorities to achieve the goals of risk reduction and a more sustainable future. The EU Civil Protection Mechanism also operates in the EU. According to Article 214 of the Lisbon Treaty, the EU has a number of obligations to prevent and respond to natural or man-made disasters worldwide. The Treaty also gives the EU authorities the power to take decisions on private enterprises [22].

3.2. Organization of the system of civil protection and response to emergency situations in EU member states

It coordinates assistance to affected countries during the crisis, including the provision of material resources and specialist equipment, the conduct of relief operations, and the establishment and operation of national workforces. The Centre coordinates cooperation between all EU member states, six additional mechanism states, the UK, its neighbours, as well as migration agencies and humanitarian organizations. The Centre operates 24 hours a day and can provide assistance in the event of natural disasters in any EU country or beyond, at the request of national authorities or UN emergency officials. A coordinated response to man-made and natural disasters at European level will avoid duplication of aid efforts and ensure that aid is tailored to the needs of those in need. The Emergency Response Coordination Centre can communicate directly with national officials in countries in need and can also coordinate the movement of supplies and equipment between countries. The emergency management system has a special portal that provides detailed information about emergencies.

It coordinates the issue of providing assistance to countries affected by emergency situations, in particular, regarding the allocation of material resources and specialized equipment, conducting expertise, and the formation and deployment of civil protection groups. The Center coordinates interaction between all EU member states, the six additional mechanism states, Great Britain, the affected country, and civil protection and humanitarian experts. The center works 24 hours a day and can provide assistance to any EU state or outside it in the event of a large-scale disaster at the request of national authorities or an authorized UN body. A coordinated response to man-made disasters and natural hazards at European level avoids duplication of aid efforts and ensures that aid is tailored to the needs of those affected. The Emergency Response Coordination Center can liaise directly with the national civil protection authorities of the country in need of assistance, as well as financially support the transport of civil protection forces and equipment to the affected country. The Emergency Response Coordination Center has its own portal, which details its activities and provides other relevant information.

In the event of a sudden attack on the territory of Hungary or armed terrorism against Hungary, the president and the government develop a defense plan to repel such an attack; possible use of the armed forces of Hungary, including the reserve forces of air defense, and foreign armed forces. The Government of Hungary, by a qualified majority of its members, may suspend the operation of certain ordinary laws as necessary, taking into account urgent needs. These measures are in effect until the moment when the parliament introduces emergency measures, a state of emergency or martial law.

Also, a state of emergency is introduced on the territory of Hungary to eliminate the consequences of natural disasters and industrial accidents that threaten the normal life of give and take.

Thus, the martial law regime in Hungary is associated with the possibility of the government temporarily suspending the operation of laws by passing decrees, to the extent necessary to resolve the crisis situation. A rather detailed regulation of the procedure for introducing martial law was also carried out in accordance with Chapter XI of the Constitution of Poland dated April 2, 1997. According to Article 238 of the Constitution of Poland, a state of emergency is declared in exceptional cases when the mechanism for the protection of constitutional law and order is insufficient to overcome threats to national security. Varieties of this special regime are martial law (introduced in case of aggression, threat of aggression by a foreign state), state of emergency (applied in cases of internal tension), state of natural disaster. All the special regimes listed above are introduced by law. In case of introduction of any of the special regimes, separate temporary restrictions on human rights may be introduced.

During the introduction of a state of emergency in Poland, the following cannot be changed: the Constitution, provisions on elections to the Diet, the Senate and local self-government bodies, the law on the election of the president of the Republic, as well as laws on the state of emergency and its types. During a state of emergency, as well as within 90 days after its cancellation, shortening the term of office of the Seimas, holding a nationwide referendum, announcing elections for the President, Seimas, Senate, or territorial self-government are inadmissible. The terms of authority of these bodies may be extended until threats to the country's security are eliminated. Appointment of elections to local self-government bodies is possible only in those regions where a state of emergency has not been declared.

The head of state submits an order on the introduction of martial law or a state of emergency, signed by the President of the Polish People's Republic, to the Diet within 48 hours. The Diet immediately considers the order of the President of Poland on the introduction of one of the listed special regimes. The Diet can cancel such an order of the President of Poland by an absolute majority of votes, if at least half of the legally established number of deputies are present at the meeting. In order to prevent the consequences of a natural disaster or technical accidents that have the nature of a natural disaster, as well as to eliminate them, the

Council of Ministers of Poland may for a certain period (no more than 30 days) introduce a state of natural disaster in part or all of the territory of Poland. This provision can be extended if the Sejm agrees.

In Spain, in the event of an external threat to the country's defense capability, the parliament can delegate to the government the right to adopt decrees. Such acts cannot regulate the activities of state institutions, rights, freedoms, duties of citizens, the position of regional autonomous associations, universal suffrage.

In Latin American countries, the president initiates "emergency" legislation and the introduction of a state of emergency and martial law throughout the country or in certain areas, usually for a long period.

For example, according to Article 72 of the Constitution of Chile, the president has the right to introduce four types of states of emergency in the country, during which the constitutional rights and freedoms of citizens are temporarily suspended. Siege (martial law), special state (ATO regime), state of emergency (in case of an internal threat) and disaster (in case of natural emergencies). The reasons for the introduction of these regimes can be the following: external war, internal war, internal upheavals, extraordinary circumstances and social disasters. All these conditions, with the exception of foreign war, are classified as internal causes. The Constitution also establishes the president's authority to declare any type of state of emergency. The head of state has the right to suspend or limit the personal freedom of citizens, the right to assembly, freedom of information and expression, the right to work, to create associations and trade unions, to introduce censorship of correspondence and messages, to limit some property rights of citizens, freedom of movement, and to carry out extradition, ban entry into the country.

Conclusions to the third chapter

Based on the above points of view, the following signs of military operations (the use of military personnel as part of the armed forces or other military formations) can be distinguished: firstly, such use is possible only in the presence of a certain international humanitarian law and domestic legal acts devoted to defense issues, a combination of factors and conditions; secondly, these factors and conditions are the legal facts of the beginning of hostilities – armed confrontation, armed conflict, use of military weapons and means of warfare. It should be noted that the authors consider it possible to conduct hostilities in peacetime, when the departments responsible for ensuring national security conduct anti-terrorist operations with the aim of destroying illegal armed groups (armed groups). It is impossible not to notice what is indicated.

Thus, activities in the field of emergency risk management and civil protection in the EU are organized according to the principles of jurisdiction and broad cooperation actions that are one of the key factors in ensuring national stability. Currently, many EU countries practice a comprehensive systemic approach to ensuring preparedness and response to a wide range of threats, according to which the issues of civil protection of the population and crisis management are considered in conjunction with other aspects of ensuring national security and stability. In general, there are certain changes in the EU's conceptual approach to ensuring sustainability, with regard to directing greater efforts to strengthening the sustainability of the Union and its members, rather than external actions and assistance to developing countries. There have also been changes regarding the strengthening of the defense and security components of the EU policy at the same time as the further development of crisis management and the provision of sustainable development.

CHAPTER 4

The Current Security Environment and the Conditions of Martial State in Ukraine

Studying the security environment, identifying dangerous trends, extremism, conflicts and threats to national security makes it possible to choose the best model for ensuring national stability and develop appropriate strategies for a modernizing state. At the same time, the existing capabilities, functions, regulatory and legal norms, the organization of national security affairs, crisis management and critical analysis of public administration allow the country to solve fragile, systemic problems in the state and society, ensuring stability, as well as making plans for its further strengthening. The analysis of these issues is of important scientific and practical importance for confirming Ukraine's ability to form a means of ensuring national stability, as well as establishing its main characteristics, patterns of stability and important aspects of national stability.

4.1. The main trends in the development of the security environment of Ukraine

Analysis of the security situation in Ukraine is important for identifying the main actions and trends that have led to changes in the global security landscape and in the cultural values of the world order. Most experts agree that global security is currently experiencing an unprecedented transformation and a decline in competitiveness. The US National Intelligence Council report "Global Trends 2040: A More Conflict-Prone World" emphasizes that the COVID-19 pandemic resembles a global crisis and the high interdependence has exposed many risks. According to experts, in the coming years and decades, the world is likely to face unprecedented challenges in many respects with cascading effects that will test the stability and adaptability of societies, states, and institutions in general [40]. The report highlights the complex challenges and trends of global development: political tensions are rising around the world, tensions are rising as state and non-state actors use new powers to challenge established norms and undermine institutions that have provided some stability in previous decades; growing disparities in economic development and competition in global markets; the inevitable aging of populations, reaching a share of the population for developing countries, Latin America, South Asia, North Africa and the Middle East; the adverse effects of climate change; the strengthening of social strata in societies, increasing distrust of authority, the creation of like-minded groups based on established or newly acquired identities; growing political instability within the state, ethnic cleansing; and the rapid development of new and innovative technologies.

The UK Ministry of Defence report, "The Strategic State of the World. The Future Begins Today," states that the world is becoming more complex and changing, and "the only certainty is that the day is already getting darker." According to the report's authors, the speed and scale of change may depend heavily on the cohesion of governments and communities. This requires good nutrition [37]. Experts have identified trends that will be observed in the next 30 years (up to 2050) and include adaptation: expanding human potential: the spread of new knowledge and technologies, on the one hand, opens up new opportunities for education and treatment, and, on the other hand, for deepening social stratification and, as a result, political conflict; change and diffusion of power: increasing tensions between Asian countries (mainly China and India) and the United States. Not all states can cope with new political and social challenges [37]. Among the trends that need to be strengthened or reduced, experts from the Ministry of Defense of the United Kingdom named: a sharp increase in the role of information: the degree of people's access to information, from the point of view of the development of computer technologies, artificial intelligence, digitalization of various aspects of life, etc. not only expand people's capabilities, but also create corresponding new risks, creating the possibility of polarization of society through social media, reducing trust in existing state institutions, the spread of cyberattacks and other crimes committed using the Internet and social networks, etc.; the development of new methods of industrialization (the First Industrial Revolution) affects all sectors of the economy and leads to social changes, social discontent and unrest due to a decrease in the number of labor and a change in its quality, as well as to disruption of people's work and leisure [37]. In addition, British experts identified trends that require further action: increasing pressure on natural resources due to climate change and human activity; unexpected changes in demographic trends in different countries, which may lead to excessive mobility, increased burden on social security and increased burden on the health of individual citizens, etc. [37].

According to the authors of the report, the greatest risks are events and circumstances that cannot be predicted. In particular, radical changes in the formation of geopolitical alliances, sudden changes in social, economic or political conditions, serious conflicts and natural disasters, trade disputes, damage to the world economy, the population, damage to the physical environment, etc. [37]. According to the head of the Swedish Security Service, what is now considered an opportunity may become a threat in the future, and events that are not more attention is needed before this happens. The expert emphasizes the importance of modern structures, not traditional ones. According to the World Economic Forum's report on "Global Risks 2021," the following are identified as risks that will arise in the next 10 years: extreme weather events, climate change, environmental degradation due to human activities, increased demand for digital energy, and discrimination and cybercrime.

The greatest threat to humanity in the next 50 years is the possibility of a new megawar with catastrophic consequences. In the modern world, the importance of gender equality and the consequences of increasing conflicts in the struggle for development are also noted in the study of the International Bank for Reconstruction and Development "World Development Report 2011. Progress, Security, Development." Experts calculate the losses suffered by both the national and global economies [8]. The authors of "The Limits to Development: Thirty Years Later" discuss the global impact of vision loss, as well as the time lag between the approach of vision loss and its public assessment 1 [26]. Given the interdependence and increasing interdependence of states, the scale of the impact of global risks on the state of national and international governance increases. The effectiveness of preventive and control measures depends largely on the ability to identify and eliminate global risks. The greatest threats to peace and stability have been identified as: Russian aggression; Chinese influence; illegal migration and human trafficking; lack of weather and weather control technologies in monitoring poverty; hybrid and other asymmetric threats, including in cyberspace; the act of providing disinformation; abuse of new drugs, etc. [29]. The European Union's Global Strategy for Foreign and Security Policy, "Looking Together, Working Together: A Stronger Europe" (2016), notes that the world is in a state of existential crisis. The document highlights the growing amount of violence, economic inequality and climate change in different parts of the world [22]. The UK National Security Strategy and the UK Department of State and Security note that in a rapidly changing globalized world, what happens abroad has a significant impact on domestic security. Japan's national security strategy reflects the following risks and challenges in the context of national security: changing balance of power and rapid development of new technologies; increasing abuse of drugs and related goods; ethnic terrorism; threats to international security (maritime, air, space, cyberspace) related to the violation of territorial integrity, the struggle for power, etc.; risks to global security and human development (inequality, poverty, the spread of chronic diseases, etc.); challenges in the context of global economic development [34]. The 2017 US national security strategy identified that the world is becoming increasingly dangerous due to a number of risks, including: the proliferation of nuclear weapons, the strengthening of global capital, publications on economic and military security, a conspiracy to distort information democracy, the activities of extremists, terrorist groups, terrorism and international crime, etc. [33]. Analysis of the security situation and the conditions for its development became the basis for the formation of strategic documents regarding Ukraine.

An important role in this position is played by the preparation of annual assessment reports and other assessment documents for the National Assembly. In particular, the overview report of the National Strategic Plan to the annual message of the President of Ukraine to the Verkhovna Rada "On the internal and external situation of Ukraine" (2020) states that "the world is simultaneously facing the threat of changes, the consequences and processes of which are difficult to predict, are the most important characteristics of the modern period" [1]. The National Security Strategy of Ukraine is a national strategy to overcome current and potential threats to security and national interests, taking into account foreign policy and domestic trends.

Among the threats associated with the global process, the following are high in particular: the impact of climate change on climate change and human evolution; uncertainties of global development and other uncertainties; increased security; the consequences of rapid technological change; the spread of violent extremism and violent crime; escalation of transatlantic tensions, disruption of the life of the population with significant human casualties and material losses, threats to the state sovereignty and territorial integrity of Ukraine. The main challenges in the development of difficult and complex situations in Ukraine include climate change and new and unexpected events, the possibility of epidemics among people and the spread of dangerous diseases among animals, degradation of the natural environment, and also water supply sources. At the same time, some of the challenges may be challenges to the national security of Ukraine or are new opportunities for development. First, it is about expressing the potential of scientific and technological development. The above-mentioned risks and challenges are serious, long-term in nature, may have significant negative consequences for society and the state, and cannot be completely eliminated. In Ukraine, even the most ambitious reforms (national security, anti-corruption) will not be successful; use of hard assets (mainly money) and their use; prevailing racial and social conditions; limited experience of state and local health care providers; impact of current and future risks on the environment; public distrust of government, etc.

4.2. The current state of martial law in the sphere of national security of Ukraine

The main problem of ensuring national security is that measures in the relevant direction are fragmentary and unsystematized, and therefore less effective. The lack of terminological and conceptual certainty regarding the provision of national stability, as well as specialized legislation, the lack of coordination in the relevant sphere – all this significantly restrains the processes of strengthening national stability, violates the main principles of its

provision (complexity, broad interaction, adaptability, predictability, reliability, awareness, readiness, mobility, redundancy, continuity, subsidiarity).

The Russian invasion of Ukraine caused extraordinary interest in international law both in professional circles and among the
general public. However, it is often a criticism of the weak appli-
cability of the norms of international law and its ineffectiveness
or obsolescence. The ongoing conflict clearly poses complex challenges to the international order, but the unprecedented response
of states and other actors has revived many norms of international law and confirmed their validity and relevance today. There
was also an unprecedented positive development of legislation in
a number of areas.

Using five examples, the author will show how the conflict in
Ukraine caused the desired development of events in selected areas of international law. First, the strong response of the international community confirmed the validity of the ban on the international use of force and the ban on the forcible seizure of territory,
while the conflicts of recent years have raised doubts as to whether
these bans still apply. Second, comprehensive economic measures
against Russia demonstrate the centrality of sanctions as a tool
for ensuring international legal order. Third, the EU activated the
Temporary Protection Directive for the first time in response to
the wave of refugees from Ukraine, which gave the impetus for
a real consideration of the much-needed reform of the refugee law
system. Fourth, states have adopted a more restrictive interpretation of the norms of international humanitarian law (IHL) and
demand stricter protection of nuclear power plants, condemning
even the threat of using nuclear weapons. And fifthly, the commission of crimes against international law in Ukraine ignited a discussion about the responsibility and the possibility of punishing
political and military representatives of Russia.

The conflict in Ukraine highlighted the importance not only of
Article 2(4) of the Charter, but also of international alliances. In
the system of international cooperation, as it has developed at the
moment, the pressure to comply with the standards is exerted by
the states themselves and the organizations that associate them.
Despite the fact that Ukraine has filed a lawsuit at the International Court of Justice of the United Nations, the proceedings may

last for years and have a difficult to predict outcome. Meanwhile, however, multilateral organizations and individual states took the reins and, using the means available to them in the international relations system, tried to force an end to the illegal situation caused by Russia. In addition to the EU, the World Trade Organization and certain countries of North America and Asia also took part in complex economic sanctions.

The strengths and weaknesses of the aforementioned program are presented below based on relevant research in Ukraine. Assessment of goals and opportunities, assessment of threats and vulnerabilities. Of course, different ministries, departments, and healthcare systems work together. In particular, in accordance with the Law of Ukraine "On National Security of Ukraine", the National Security Strategy of Ukraine is developed in accordance with the strategic action plan to overcome existing and potential threats to national security and national sovereignty of Ukraine in order to take into account foreign policy and domestic events, a comprehensive analysis of the security and defense sector has been conducted [64]. When developing programs within the framework of national policy and international law to meet the needs of Ukraine, ministries and departments should conduct a strategic analysis in their areas of responsibility, identifying specific risks and challenges. In addition, in accordance with Article 68 of the Strategic Plan of Ukraine for National Security (2020), reports are prepared on the state of Ukraine's national security based on the analysis of the national strategic plan for the national security strategy [75]. Reports on the assessment of the national strategic plan to the annual message of the President of Ukraine to the Verkhovna Rada "On the internal and external situation of Ukraine" contain a comprehensive assessment of the current state of societies, as well as an analysis of these and other issues in the field of foreign policy, economy, social relations, etc. It is possible to determine the main structures of the state and society. At the same time, the identification of risks and opportunities is important for the formulation, adoption and implementation of strategic approaches to the consequences of climate change; the level of management necessary to address issues in this area; reducing the exchange of information necessary for making state decisions, etc. Strategic analysis, determining priorities for ensuring national stability, measures of preparedness to respond to a complex of threats and crisis situations and further strategic planning.

Coordination and coordination of activities at the national, regional and local levels in the field of anti-crisis management poses significant challenges in the context of effective cultural changes. The ability to try to respond quickly to complex situations in Ukraine still remains limited. First of all, this is due to the lack of parental commitment, duty, and especially their commitment to the organization.

In addition, research projects are being carried out in the field of development of security and defense of Ukraine, in which previous experience is analyzed. Currently, scientific agreements between all regions of the security and defense sector of Ukraine have been established and are being implemented. The Ukraine-NATO Platform has also been created to study the Ukrainian experience of fighting insurgents. The results of exercises and international cooperation, as well as the analysis of experience gained as a result of previous events, are used, in particular, in the development of program documents: National Security Strategy, Ukraine under the auspices of occupation – NATO, commissions, as well as other documents of the past in the field of national security and defense. Historical experience can also draw important conclusions regarding strategies and tactics that ensure national stability. It should be noted that in the USSR during the war there was great interest in issues of civil defense and stabilization of the national economy. Various civil protection measures have been developed and implemented, as well as measures to ensure the state's preparedness for emergencies and martial law.

The results of the next wave of the National Survey of Civic Activity called "Join!" Conducted in the spring of 2021, showed that the level of participation of Ukrainian citizens in active civic activities was very low: only 6.8 % attended peaceful rallies, compared to 8 % engaged in construction or building houses, cars, or a neighborhood committee. Another 8.1 % reported being interviewed in person, by phone, or online. Only 4 % of respondents indicated that they actively participated in events last year, and another 13 % indicated that they participated in such events from time to time. Ukrainians voluntarily participate in the life of their communities – this is reported by a third (33 %).

Only 7.4 % of respondents said that they regularly hold gatherings at home, on the street, or in the neighborhood. At the same time, two-thirds of respondents noted that they have neither the time (33.3 %) nor the interest (31.7 %) to participate in such events [17]. These results are based on a study conducted in March 2021 by the Social Sciences Service of the Razumkov Center on the situation in the country, the institutional structure of society and politicians, and the electoral capacity of citizens. Most often directed at civil servants (officials) (80 %), expressed in the legislative body (generally constitutional) (79 %), the Verkhovna Rada of Ukraine (77.5 %), the Government of Ukraine (76 %), the Supreme Law on Combating Corruption (73 %), political parties (71 %), the Prosecutor's Office (71 %), Commercial Bank (70 %), NABU (70 %), the Supreme Court (69 %), the Constitution of Ukraine (69 %), the Administrative Offenses Office (68 %), the National Agency for the Prevention of Corruption (NACP) (68 %), local administration (66 %), the President of Ukraine (60 %). The highest level of trust in the Armed Forces of Ukraine (they are trusted by 70 % of the population), furthermore, a high level of trust is shown by institutions (65 %), the Church (64 %), state security bodies (63 %), the state border guard (60 %), employees of the national executive power of Ukraine (56 %), mayors of cities (towns, villages) where the victims live (56 %), organizations (55 %), public administration (53 %), urban infrastructure (towns, villages) where the respondents live (51 %). A similar study conducted in June 2018 by the Razumkov Center's Social Sciences Service showed that among the institutions of the state and society, citizens trust institutions the most (65.2 % of respondents), the church (61.1 %). Armed Forces of Ukraine (57.2 %), volunteer units (50 %), State Emergency Service (51.1 %), State Border Service (50.7 %), National Guard of Ukraine (48.6 %), National Security and Defense Council (43.4 %) – the number of respondents who believe in these institutions is significantly (statistically) greater than those who would not trust them. For comparison, the President of Ukraine is trusted by 13.8 % of respondents, while 80.6 % do not trust him; Government – respectively 13.7 % and 80.7 %; Verkhovna Rada – 10.3 % and 85.6 %; National Bank – 14.1 % and 76.2 %; The Supreme Court – 10.6 % and 75.2 %. Trust in state institutions (officials) was expressed by 8.6 % of the surveyed respondents against 85.3 % of distrust [14]. Scientists of the Razumkov Center distinguish the following trends in the political orientations of Ukrainian citizens: distrust of the political and political system and low interest in politics (61 %) [15]. Similar symbols are widespread in Europe, especially in Latvia, Bulgaria and Hungary.

The Verkhovna Rada of Ukraine adopted the law on the approval of the presidential decree on the extension of martial law in Ukraine for 90 days from February 14 to May 13. 355 MPs voted for the legislative act "On the continuation of martial law in Ukraine".

Thus, martial law in Ukraine was extended until May 13. On February 24, 2022, the Russian invasion began. On the same day, martial law was declared in the country and a state of emergency was declared until March 26. Subsequently, the Resolution of the Verkhovna Rada extended the martial law and general operations until April 25, May 25, August 23, November 21, 2022, as well as February 19, May 20, August 18, November 15, 2023 and November 14, 2024.

Thus, a systemic mechanism for ensuring national security, which should introduce measures to strengthen the autonomy of security policy and implement the basic principles of the survival of the state and society in a constantly changing security environment, in addition to eliminating the ideologies that form the basis of the state and society, has not yet been created in Ukraine. At the same time, there are great opportunities to strengthen and develop the stability of the state and society. Based on the above, it can be argued that the need to develop a law on ensuring national stability in Ukraine is fully justified. Given the limited resources of the state and the available resources and mechanisms for stabilizing national interests and problems, taking into account the available resource connections, it is desirable to build such an infrastructure that will provide clarity in various areas of management regarding the employment of resources for the needs of agriculture. Given the importance of issues and objects in ensuring national security and national stability, organizational strategies can develop related systems as subsystems of strategic planning or related systems. In the future, it is desirable to modernize and combine these systems into a single comprehensive system for ensuring national security and stability.

4.3. Systemic problems of national security in Ukraine

4.3.1. Problems of defining the goals and tasks of ensuring martial law in the strategic documents of Ukraine

To determine political vectors, goals and objectives within the framework of ensuring national security, state strategic and program documents are focused primarily on national security strategies. Such articles are critical of the role and place of the state in the modern world, its national character, legitimacy and goals, as well as the powers, abilities and responsibilities to protect against external and internal threats. The relevant legislation determines the policy and procedures for ensuring national stability, and the provision of relevant strategies and program documents can determine the direction of its development or improvement. Today, the main legislative task, according to which priorities in the field of national security and defense are implemented, including the development of relevant strategic documents, is the Law of Ukraine "On National Security of Ukraine" [64]. According to clause 15 of part 1 of the Law on National Development, the national development of Ukraine, the actual organization of development, planning, implementation and support of the activities and activities of the Republic of Ukraine are entrusted to state institutions, it is the responsibility of security and defense sector stakeholders to determine the capabilities of the state based on the security situation and taking into account the economic aspects of investments.

The purpose of cooperation in the field of national security and defense is to determine the structures of the defense and defense sector, capabilities, strategies, development plans, resource management and their effective distribution in terms of strategies for ensuring the implementation of state policy in these areas. Cooperation in the field of national security and defense is carried out according to the following criteria: 1) respect for national law and international law of Ukraine; 2) openness of information about national civilian control, state policy, strategic documents, goals, priorities and measures in the field of security and defense, transparency and accountability in the use of resources; 3) transparency, integrity, fairness in the field of security and defense, taking into account institutional and operational policies through national strategies, plans and priority documents; 4) the timing and compliance of decisions taken to protect the national interests of Ukraine (parts one and two of Article 25 of the Law). This is about continuity with all other priorities in the field of national security and defense. The National Security Strategy of Ukraine operates on the principles of national defense, security, economy and intellectual property using mechanisms of public-private partnership, as well as on the basis of international consultations, finances and materials with the right to cooperation (part three of Article 26 of the Law).

The Treaty enshrines the principles of the National Security Strategy of Ukraine, including the principles of security, as well as the principles that are built on its basis, namely: the Military and Defense Strategy of Ukraine, Cybersecurity of Ukraine, the Ministry of Foreign Affairs of Ukraine, the Ministry of Public Affairs and Civil Affairs, the Ministry of Foreign Affairs of the Defense Industry of Ukraine, and the State Secret Service. In accordance with the law, the National Security Strategy of Ukraine defines: 1) the priorities of Ukraine's national security and national security management, goals, principles of the state's interests in the field of national security; 2) existing and immediate threats to the national sovereignty and territorial integrity of Ukraine, taking into account foreign and domestic circumstances; 3) the main foundations of the state's foreign policy strategy, such as ensuring its national interests and security; 4) policies and programs that contribute to the improvement and development of security and defense operations; and 5) equipment necessary for the performance of work. Until 2018, the legal basis for the national security of Ukraine was the Law of Ukraine "On the Fundamentals of Ensuring the National Security of Ukraine" [67], which defines the national security rights of Ukraine, cyber law and the defense of Ukraine and the Military Doctrine of Ukraine. Republic as a mandatory document and as the basis for formulating operations on the basis of state national limits law. Requirements for the procedure for producing such documents, their terms and conditions are not established by this law, but in practice they are requirements of national security and are challenged by the primary principles and functions of the state legislative branch.

Strategic investments in the relevant sphere of s put into effect by the Constitution of Ukraine "On the Prospects of the Defense Plan" [66]. The first National Security Strategy of Ukraine was adopted in 2007 [93]. The document outlined a wide range of challenges to national security, many of which remain relevant today. The latest national security strategy was approved by the President of Ukraine in 2012 [89]. It highlighted the changes that have occurred in the security situation in Ukraine during this period, as well as the challenges that have arisen in the field of protection of the individual, community and state.

Since Ukraine was not and is not a set of international military-political alliances, it relied exclusively on self-determination, and this required a radical redistribution of state power and a revision of its priorities in the field of national security and defense. Given the significant changes in the security situation, the National Security Strategy of Ukraine was on the agenda. In addition, under the legislation in force at that time, Ukraine was forced to maintain its territorial integrity without interference, and the Russian Federation recognized territorial borders that, according to the 2014 agreement, were incompatible with peace or national sovereignty. In 2015, a new programmatic framework for the National Security Strategy of Ukraine was approved [88]. The document explicitly states that the greatest threat to Ukraine at the moment is the invasion of the Russian Federation, the purpose of which is to destabilize the Ukrainian economy and undermine socio-political stability, taking measures that could lead to the collapse of the Ukrainian state. The main goals of the regime within the framework of stabilizing the national identity of Ukraine are determined: returning territorial sovereignty to Ukraine; creating an advanced investment and defense sector; increasing the defense capability of the state; reforming and developing intelligence, intelligence and law enforcement agencies; reforming public administration; establishing a new quality of anti-corruption measures; ensuring greater security in the EU and a special partnership with NATO. It also identified a number of important issues in the main areas of national security: foreign policy, economic, development, information, cyber, environmental, protection of foreign resources. The strategy clearly defines the processes of national development and gives them a comprehensive assessment. In addition, these measures were coordinated with the provisions of other regulatory and legal documents of the state – the provisions of the Coalition Agreement, the Sustainable Development Goals "Ukraine – 2020." However, three important state documents remain unconsidered. The Sustainable Development Strategy "Ukraine – 2020," approved by the Decree of the President of Ukraine of January 12, 2015 [94], provides for the implementation of 62 reforms and measures aimed at popularizing the "European way of life." in Ukraine and Ukraine has gained a prominent place in the world. Thus, the previous documents of the National Security Strategy of Ukraine, adopted in 2007, 2012 and 2015, described current external and internal threats and threats, as well as their predecessors – constraints in the field of national security. However, the scale of implementation of these documents was relatively low, and some efforts (in particular, on the fight against corruption, on the reform of security and defense agencies and public administration) were in some cases repeated. In addition to the lack of political will for change, this situation was largely due to the lack of clear commitments to implement the Strategy in many areas of national security (with the exception of defense and later cybersecurity). The rules for implementing strategic planning documents were informal, reporting procedures on achieved results, specifications and instructions were not established, and they were not evaluated to ensure that they meet the goals of strategic planning. The Law of Ukraine "On the State Security of Ukraine" [64] adopted in 2018 created a legal framework to create a new quality of the national security system in accordance with the needs of the current situation. The event was attended by experienced businessmen, representatives of state authorities and civil society. The development of this agreement takes into account the laws and policies of NATO and the EU, which are within the framework of ensuring national sovereignty. This framework law determines the legal basis of the sphere of public relations with the consistency and non-contradiction of its provisions in other legal and regulatory frameworks.

In accordance with the current National Security Strategy of Ukraine, "Human Security – Homeland Security" takes into account the practical consequences of strategic planning and management

strategies in the security sector, as well as the lessons learned from countering hybrid aggression by Ukraine. The National Security Strategy of Ukraine is based on the following basic principles:
– deterrence – development of defense and security capabilities to prevent armed aggression against Ukraine;
– resilience – the ability of society and the state to quickly adapt to changes in the security environment and maintain sustainable functioning, in particular by minimizing external and internal vulnerabilities;
– interaction – development of strategic relations with key foreign partners, primarily with the European Union and NATO and their member states, the United States of America, pragmatic cooperation with other states and international organizations based on the national interests of Ukraine [91].

The difficulties specified in the resolution of the National Security and Defense Council of Ukraine dated August 20, 2021, were partially resolved by the Decree "On the Organization of Territorial Integration of State Stability", which approved the Concept of Stabilization, including the National Stabilization Process. is going to resolve the Concept of Implementation of the Legislative Framework of Ukraine and other problems in the field of ensuring the national stability of Ukraine.

The State Emergency Service conducted a comprehensive analysis of fire, human and natural hazards, their monitoring and response, exchanged information with other states to disseminate relevant knowledge and experience, the Ministry of Internal Affairs of Ukraine, together with the State Security Service, the State Border Guard Service of Ukraine, the Administration of the State Border Guard of Ukraine and the Ukrainian State Security Service, undertook a project to strengthen the national education system by ensuring the security of the armed forces. The Main Directorate of National Police of Ukraine has successfully created a single communication center "102" to receive information about events and a dispatcher service that carries out centralized management of orders in the territory; at the same time, a mobile application was launched, which aims to ensure the accessibility of streets throughout the state.

In the IV stage of 2020, Ukraine launched a comprehensive strategic planning program at the national level based on the provisions of the Ukrainian National Treaty [111]. These are the Strategic Plan for Human Development, the Strategy for Military Security of Ukraine, the Strategy for Public Security and Civil Protection of Ukraine, the Strategy for the Development of the Electric Power Industry of Ukraine, the Strategy for Economic Development, the Strategy for Energy Security, Environmental Protection and Approaches to Climate Change, Biosecurity and Biological Mechanisms, Information Technologies, Ukrainian Cyber Affairs, Foreign Affairs, State Affairs, Integrated Border Management Affairs, Food Affairs, State Affairs.

The Sectoral Security Strategy is a priority document of the second level, a systematic review of the program to achieve identified social risks and priority results (over a five-year period). They consider, but do not predict, current and future climate change, the state of the security environment, and national strategic priorities. These methods are described in detail in the following sections of the manual. At the same time, the uncertainty of the conceptual foundations in the formulation of means of ensuring national stability in Ukraine during the development of strategic planning documents at the national level did not lead to the creation of clearly necessary measures in financing the upper sector. There is also no correlation between state documents of measures to ensure national stability and security in Ukraine [115].

The National Intelligence Agenda for 2021–2025 was amended [97], and as of September 1, 2021, only six articles were approved: Military Strategy of Ukraine [83], Personnel Support Program [77], Economic Defense Program of Ukraine, and for the period up to 2025 [74], Defense-Industrial Cooperation Program [80], Cybersecurity Strategy of Ukraine [76], and Foreign Policy Strategy of Ukraine [86]. The issue of finalizing and implementing the National Security Strategy of Ukraine remains more relevant than ever. In order to fulfill the additional commitments set out in this document, it is important to make sure that the relevant commitments do not exist simply as another declaration.

It is important to note that this meeting provides an opportunity to discuss issues related to relations between the two countries. 335 deputies voted for the continuation of the military competitions announced on February 24, 2022, and no one was against. Martial law was extended until May 13, and the occupation continued.

The vote for the decree was essentially just a formality, since none of the Ukrainian political elites supports the abolition of martial law during the war. The extension of martial law means, among other things, that the presidential elections in Ukraine will not be held on the official Friday of March this year. Thus, President Zelensky's term of office will automatically increase, but his five-year term will end in May. The elections will be held after the end of martial law. The Ukrainian parliament is to consider the draft law on the Law on Registration and Prevention of War, which was discussed in the first reading, which is to clarify the rules for registering war and strengthen various measures to continue the fight against it even more, supporting the Russian invasion. substantial military state.

The key provision of the bill is the reduction of the age limit for those who can go to war from 27 to 25 years. The new bill retains key provisions of the original bill, including electronic notification of malfunctions and stricter penalties for those who violate mobilization rules. The provisions of the previous provisions of the bill, which concern Ukrainians living abroad, are also considered relevant, since citizens who have a passport must provide documents for military registration. To travel abroad, Ukrainians aged 18 to 60 must present their first identity card with an exit mark.

Any attempt to avoid conscription may lead to criminal prosecution and legal actions, including freezing bank accounts and assets, driving and consumption restrictions. The law provides for demobilization after 36 months – this text of the law caused heated discussion in Ukraine: relatives of fighters still fighting at the front demanded to clarify the exact terms of their treatment.

According to the results of the analysis, it can be concluded that institutional, organizational and legal uncertainty significantly slow down the process of forming a national identity in Ukraine. In addition, the failure of Ukraine's policy at the strategic planning stage creates a risk of inconsistency and incomplete implementation of measures to strengthen national stability.

4.3.2. Terminological uncertainty in the sphere of ensuring martial law in Ukraine

There is a terminological uncertainty in various strategic plans and documents on state cooperation (in particular, the National Security Strategy of Ukraine (2020) [75], the annual national strategy under the auspices of the Ukraine-NATO Commission for 2020 [72] (hereinafter referred to as the NSP-2020)). In accordance with the Regulation on the National Development Plan of Ukraine dated December 31, 2020 14.09.2020 34. In 2021, the total number of articles approved by the Procedure for Stabilizing Priority Actions in the Sphere of National Security and Defense, the development priorities of which are determined by the National Security Strategy of Ukraine, amounted to 12 out of 15 important steps in the national stability program. However, since the national stabilization policy of Ukraine has not yet been formulated, there are many problems with the use of weapons in the region, which is critical to achieving its goals. It should be noted that serious developments in the field of national stability have occurred only recently – in the Concept of the Formation of National Stability, approved by the Decree of the President of Ukraine "National Independence and Defense Capability".

However, there have been no changes in the law that would allow agricultural use of natural territories. A detailed analysis of the Constitution of Ukraine, in particular the Constitution of Ukraine "On National Security of Ukraine," "On Defense of Ukraine," "On the Armed Forces of Ukraine," "On Combating Terrorism," "On the Security Services of Ukraine," as well as the National Security Program of Ukraine, RNP-2020, RNP-2021, State Level Development Program. For 2021–2027 several conclusions can be drawn [11], "Poverty" and many other terms did not have the meaning that is widely used in the field of national development, which led to the creation and implementation of natural processes. Secondly, in various regulatory and legal documents in Ukraine, various definitions related to integrity are mentioned or given, but they have a specific meaning, since they relate to different spheres (industries) related, and therefore, specific characteristics of their application are needed. for clarity. The resolution of the State Security and Defense Council of Ukraine of August

20, 2021 refers to the "creation of a system of state stability". In particular, concepts related to peace in certain areas are used in the following regulatory and legal frameworks of Ukraine: Concepts for the creation of a state apparatus for responding to disasters [96] ("disaster safety," "community safety"); Decree of the President of Ukraine No. 722 [98] of September 30, 2019 "On the Sustainable Development Goals of Ukraine for the period up to 2030" ("Historical sustainability of the city"); National Development Plan-2020 ("economic stability," "social stability," "growth stability," "corruption," "healthy networks," "healthy society," "healthy communication," "healthy governance"); National Development Plan-2021 ("social stability," "economic stability," "national stability policy," "inflation stability," etc.); State Development Plans for 2021–2027 ("countering disasters," "improving the quality of life," "response to water shortages"), etc. Several regulatory and legal documents on Ukraine, especially regarding the National Security Strategy (2020), National Development Plan (2020), and National Development Plan (2021). It should be noted that these and other regulatory documents in Ukraine are used in the sense of "law ensuring national stability," which is an organizational and regulatory process that controls the activities of legal entities within a complex model and national identity. Fourth, the concepts of "viability" and "reliability" seem to be present in some Ukrainian legal proceedings, which are closer to the concepts of "truthfulness." As a rule, they are based on certain characteristics of the technical system and resistance to certain threats. In particular, the concept of "term" is used in the Transmission Systems Code [46], the rules for the service of ships in the Navy, based on the Armed Forces of Ukraine [52], the Order on Lifeboats of Inland Navigation Vessels [44], and the Rules for the Protection of Workers during Shipbuilding and Shipbuilding Works [59]. The laws of Ukraine include "On the Defense of Ukraine" [65], "On Combating Terrorism" [35], the Strategy of the National Defense Strategy of Ukraine (2020), RNP-2020, RNP-2021 "On Survival". Fifth, in various regulatory and legal documents on Ukraine, other terms that affirm national stability are irregularly used, in particular, "force," "threat," "readiness."

Specific references to the term "force" used in certain areas are found, in particular, in the following documents: Procedure for Maintaining the Defense Department by the Ministry of Defense [54]; Measures for conducting national anti-terrorist reviews [70]; defense-industrial cooperation program [55]; There are notable differences in all aspects of admission of students to state and public educational institutions for obtaining complete general secondary education, deductions and tuition fees [53], etc. Specific definitions of the term "distance" (including "distance" and in risk assessment sentences) are given, in particular, in the instructions for conducting risk checks in the State Border Guard Service of Ukraine [45]; instructions and information systems for providers of electronic trust services and their various registered places [37]; concepts for combating terrorism in Ukraine [62], etc. These agreements also have their implications for the future. In addition, the National Security Strategy of Ukraine (2020) uses the "pillars" and their related elements in a context that does not have a formal definition. Specific definitions of the term "readiness" are given (including in phrases), for example, in the regulation on aviation search and rescue in Ukraine [58]; instructions on lifeboats for inland navigation vessels [44]; Requirements for the organization of physical defense personnel, personnel for accounting and control of nuclear materials in emergency and crisis situations [42], etc., "On the State of Ukraine," as well as in the National Defense Strategy of Ukraine (2020), In the RNP-2020, RNP-2021, 2021–2027 the term "ready" and its definition were used without bias. It is noted above that the laws and regulatory legal acts of Ukraine relating to peace enforcement procedures do not correspond to the diversity and contradictions of the definitions used in the labor literature do not contribute to a unified understanding of the processes of public administration related to the state. This clarifies the issue of the compliance of the content of the concept in establishing national standards for establishing terms used in various regulatory legal frameworks.

4.3.3. Problems in the field of organizational maintenance of martial law

As world experience shows, effective mechanisms for ensuring national stability are largely decentralized, and decisions on regional measures are made at very narrow levels. At the same time, it is important to have uniform and understandable rules, policies and procedures for all stakeholders at different stages of the peace process. Ultimately, this is done at a high level, which is determined by each country separately. In countries with a parliamentary form of government, this function is usually performed by the government.

One of the main problems in implementing coordination and control mechanisms in the field of ensuring national security is the distribution of powers on the ground between different branches of Ukrainian government (mainly between the President of Ukraine, the National Security and Defense Council and the Cabinet of Ministers of Ukraine), which exists, makes it more difficult to develop a coordinated functional structure for managing national security and stability than a centralized one. And as noted, the parallel operation of several one-dimensional solutions increases the complexity, and also increases the risk of system failure and failure [2].

According to the Constitution of Ukraine "On National Security of Ukraine" (Article 13), the leadership in the field of national security and defense is exercised by the President of Ukraine with the exercise of all his legislative powers [64]. According to Article 107 of the Constitution of Ukraine, the State Security and Defense Council of Ukraine organizes and controls the activities of the national security and defense apparatus. According to Part One of Article 14 of the Constitution of Ukraine, the National Security and Defense Committee of Ukraine carries out activities in the field of national security and defense. At the same time, Part Two of Article 14 of the Law establishes that in the event of war or emergency situations, in special circumstances, as well as in situations that pose a threat to the national security of Ukraine – in the field of agriculture. The NSDC of Ukraine organizes the activities of investors, considers proposals for the application of specific measures of economic and other policies.

And in a separate case, in accordance with Part Three of Article 14 of the Constitution, a higher collegiate strategic body of the main leadership of the state defense may be established. At the same time, the role of state authorities in coordinating the activities of state authorities in countering threats, ensuring readiness or restoring full-fledged work after an emergency for the NSDC of Ukraine is not clearly defined. In accordance with Article 116 of the Constitution of Ukraine, the Cabinet of Ministers of Ukraine, in particular, directs and coordinates the activities of ministers and other executive authorities, the defense and national security forces of Ukraine, public security, and the fight against crime. Article 6 of the Law of Ukraine "On Civil Defense of Ukraine" stipulates that coordination of activities on civil protection issues is determined by the State Security and Defense Council of Ukraine and the Cabinet of Ministers of Ukraine within the framework of the Intersection at different levels for the integration of production, organizational and institutional activities related to the central and institutional dimensions of functional power, technogenic and environmental integrity, protection of individuals and groups, prevention of disasters and response to them – a departmental commission is being formed. In particular, the Cabinet of Ministers of Ukraine creates a state commission on arms control. At the same time, civil protection is defined by law as a function of the state, which serves to prevent such crimes, eliminate their consequences and, in particular, reduce the cost of time and money in real time [22]. Thus, the tasks related to the activities of various state institutions in the field of national sovereignty and civil rights of the people, in accordance with the Constitution, are distributed between the Cabinet of Ministers of Ukraine and the National Security and Defense Council of Ukraine.

The organizational and regulatory functions of health care systems cover the entire region of the country, many health care systems have functional and regional subsystems. Each of them is based on the principles of legislation, centralization of management, unity of command, coordination, coherence, adequate risk management, provision of basic infrastructure, in particular local self-government bodies, etc.

The main functions of the co these systems generally protect the following:

a) the population from natural, man-made, environmental, biological, chemical, radioactive, social, terrorist, military and other environmental threats and extreme conditions;

b) life support activities of the state and society, including territorial activities related to energy supply, food, drinking water, etc., as well as rehabilitation and rehabilitation, public safety, tele-communications and radio communications, cybersecurity, agri-cultural communications, housing, and public safety, etc.; and c) increasingly dispersed species that are present in the range of vertebrate and invertebrate species. Based on the analysis of spe-cific aspects of key strategies and policies of state security, suf-ficient to protect individuals and states from extreme threats and extremism perform the main functions [12]. National mechanisms for responding to various threats and challenges have been cre-ated (a unified civil protection mechanism of Ukraine; an emer-gency medical assistance mechanism; prevention, response and response to terrorist attacks and the state apparatus for eliminat-ing their consequences, the National Cyber Security Strategy of Ukraine), which performs both functions at the national, regional and local levels, has a recognition of a limited format, which is somewhat confusing. At the same time, it is legally correct to study risk management strategies and policies, respond to threats, cri-ses and emergencies and subsequent retaliatory measures.

Several liaison agencies and interagency groups work in a small group of different districts. Table 4.1 summarizes the vari-ous national liaisons according to the Ukrainian Constitution. At the same time, as can be seen on the right, direct connections (depicted by solid lines) are established only between one system, while between the others there are only formal (logical) connec-tions (depicted by dotted lines).

Taking into account the procedural analysis of the provisions of Article 24, Article 25, Article 2 of the Civil Protection Code of Ukraine [22] and Article 2, Article 3 of the Constitution of Ukraine "Fighting Terrorism" [35], it can be assumed that the emergency situation is caused, among other things, by uncertainty. Measures to ensure preparedness and response to such situations are pro-vided for by the state policy on civil protection and the state policy on preventing, responding to and eliminating the consequences of terrorist acts. The powers of regional and local commissions on the protection of the technogenic and natural environment and emer-gencies include situations, as well as local commissions on combat-ing terrorism under the supervision of the SBU hub. In addition, the situation caused by illegal activities poses a serious threat to the life or health of citizens. Therefore, emergency medicine issues

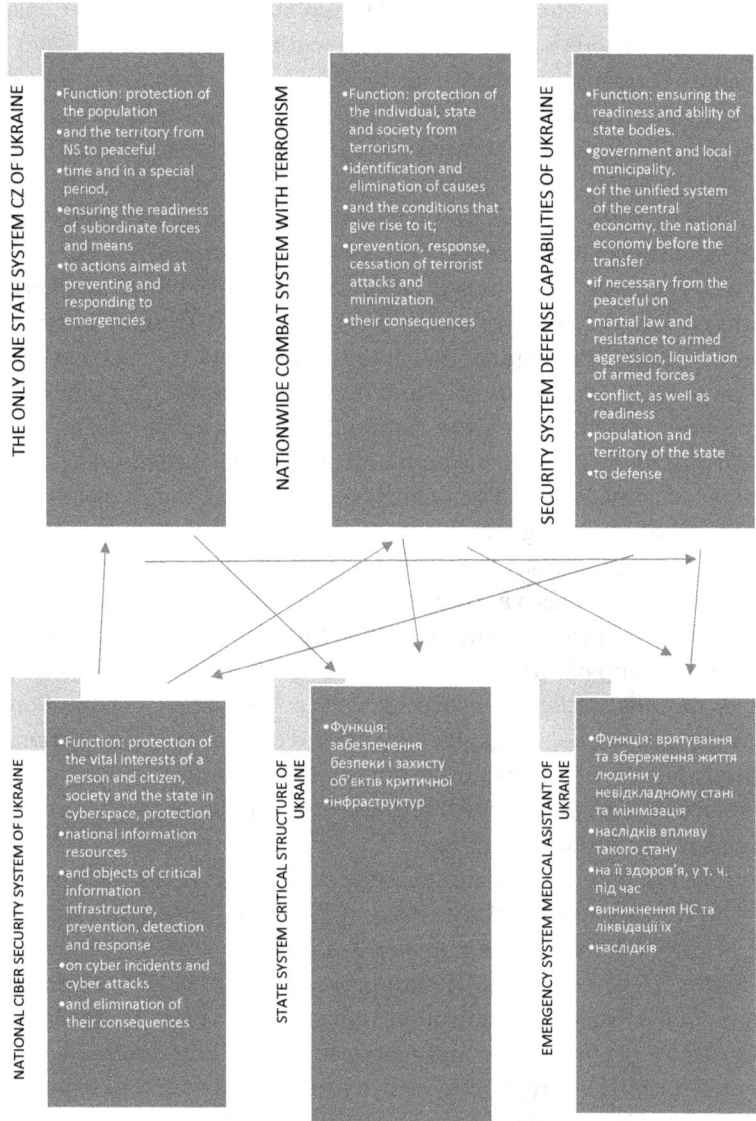

THE ONLY ONE STATE SYSTEM CZ OF UKRAINE
- Function: protection of the population
- and the territory from NS to peaceful
- time and in a special period,
- ensuring the readiness of subordinate forces and means
- to actions aimed at preventing and responding to emergencies

NATIONWIDE COMBAT SYSTEM WITH TERRORISM
- Function: protection of the individual, state and society from terrorism,
- identification and elimination of causes
- and the conditions that give rise to it;
- prevention, response, cessation of terrorist attacks and minimization
- their consequences

SECURITY SYSTEM DEFENSE CAPABILITIES OF UKRAINE
- Function: ensuring the readiness and ability of state bodies.
- government and local municipality,
- of the unified system of the central economy, the national economy before the transfer
- if necessary from the peaceful on
- martial law and resistance to armed aggression, liquidation of armed forces
- conflict, as well as readiness
- population and territory of the state
- to defense

NATIONAL CIBER SECURITY SYSTEM OF UKRAINE
- Function: protection of the vital interests of a person and citizen, society and the state in cyberspace, protection
- national information resources
- and objects of critical information infrastructure, prevention, detection and response
- on cyber incidents and cyber attacks
- and elimination of their consequences

STATE SYSTEM CRITICAL STRUCTURE OF UKRAINE
- Функція: забезпечення безпеки і захисту об'єктів критичної
- інфраструктур

EMERGENCY SYSTEM MEDICAL ASISTANT OF UKRAINE
- Функція: врятування та збереження життя людини у невідкладному стані та мінімізація
- наслідків впливу такого стану
- на її здоров'я, у т. ч. під час
- виникнення НС та ліквідації їх
- наслідків

Figure 4.1. Scheme of interrelationships between state-wide systems in the field of response to threats and emergency situations in Ukraine

Source: developed by the author.

should be included in the investigation. At the same time, the principle of intervention in crisis situation with cascading effects and the term "crisis situation" are not defined by Ukrainian legislation.

The interpretation of all possible threats and information on responding to emergencies has not been established. At the same
time, measures are taken within the framework of certain areas
(cybersecurity, counterterrorism, etc.), but they are not systemic.
Currently, the situational and crisis centers of individual ministries and departments are not united into a single network. This
complicates the creation of catalogs and databases necessary for
analysis, planning and monitoring in the field of national security.
The incompleteness and inconsistency of interdepartmental interaction in the field of ensuring national security and stability does
not contribute to a comprehensive interdisciplinary approach to
resolving the dynamics of a multi-profile and highly problematic
situation. Legal regulation of violent extremism is widespread in
various legal and regulatory frameworks of Ukraine. It is obvious
that before introducing systemic mechanisms for ensuring national stability in Ukraine, it is necessary to assess the positions,
roles and responsibilities of the entities involved in ensuring this
stability, especially state and local governments, enterprises and
organizations, as well as the consideration of civil cases, as well as
social, peacetime, emergency situations, wartime, etc., the laws of
their various subjects.

4.3.4. The imperfection of the risk and capacity assessment system in the conditions of martial law in Ukraine

Currently, Ukrainian legislation does not define a full cycle of
military actions in the field of national security, which includes
a periodic assessment of options and threats, security capabilities, deterrence and containment, measures to ensure the stability of the state, individual enterprises and groups, groups and
communities, as well as society. preparation of state strategies
and planning documents. Most of these studies are not coordinated with each other, and some are not limited at all [11]. Today,
Ukrainian ministries and departments are working to resolve
conflicts and risks in their areas of responsibility, using a variety
of mechanisms, policies and tools. The main difficulty is that the
test results obtained in this way are difficult, and often impossible, to compare.

Existing methodological shortcomings of investigations based on the experience of past events are transformed into new conclusions that were not previously available. The lack of a comprehensive analysis of the security and defense sectors and their interconnected stakeholders remains incomplete. According to Article 1 of Article 1 of the Constitution of Ukraine, the critical department of security and defense is the assessment of means and resources for the activities of security and defense partners, based on the results of which technical documents are developed and specified. and protected, and measures are taken to acquire the capabilities necessary to perform current and priority tasks are implemented in the context of [64]. Article 27 of the Law establishes the procedure for reviewing the rehabilitation program and the procedure for its implementation.

Measures for conducting critical tests are not defined, and therefore in operation during the testing of individual subsystems of the security and defense sector of Ukraine (defense, public defense and civil protection, defense-industrial complex, intelligence agency, a possible imbalance of Ukraine), a comprehensive state strategy for countering terrorism, state information systems on cybercrime, information systems etc., as well as a comparison of their reliability. Interdisciplinary cooperation and scientific results are important in this area. Given the problems of terminological and methodological uncertainty, it is difficult to understand how such an analysis can capture the strengths necessary to ensure full democratic integration, even in relation to specific areas and goals. As of August 1, 2021, the following assessments of the national security system of Ukraine have been completed: Defense Assessment – a report on the results of the assessment approved by the Ministry of National Security and Defense of Ukraine and entered into force on March 24, 2020, through Directive No. 106/2020 of 1991 [82]; Inspection of the Intelligence Agencies of Ukraine – a report on the results of the inspection published by the decision of the State Security and Defense Council of Ukraine, which was adopted by the President of Ukraine on March 23, 2021; National Review of the Results of the Anti-Terrorist Operation – a report on the results of the review published by the decision of the National Security and Defense Council of Ukraine dated June 17, 2021, No. 251/2021; The report on the results of the exercises authorized by the Decree of the President of Ukraine No. 168 of April 21, 2021, was published by the decision of the National Security and Defense Council /2021 [78]. The Law of Ukraine "On National Defense of Ukraine" requires: the verification of national defense and civil protection was not completed on time – by the decision of the National Security and Defense Council of Ukraine of December 29, 2020. Implementation in accordance with the Decree of the President of Ukraine No. 597/2020 [85] measures taken by the authorized bodies and the Ministry of Internal Affairs of Ukraine within three months (until March 29, 2021) to complete the analysis and submit a report to the National Security and Defense Council of Ukraine as an approved procedure; verification of the state of cybersecurity of critical information systems, state information systems and information, the need for protection of which is established by law, as well as the verification mechanism established by Resolution No. 1176 [56] Resolution of the Cabinet of Ministers of Ukraine dated November 11, 2020 [56], which has not yet been considered, the decision of the National Security and Defense Council of Ukraine dated May 16, 2019, which entered into force by the Decree of the President of Ukraine, remains as such, which has not entered into force.

At the same time, the Cybersecurity Strategy of Ukraine emphasizes the importance of developing a national cybersecurity infrastructure [84]. Thus, it can be stated that the measures of the National Security Strategy of Ukraine (2020) are based on the results of a comprehensive analysis of strategic activities in the field of national security and defense in accordance with NATO policies, and procedures, have not been fully implemented. It is also of concern that some inspection reports were subsequently or simultaneously recognized as priorities within the framework of local national security. This may mean that the consequences of the intervention were not fully taken into account.

The activities of the general network of situational centers should develop institutional and analytical processes, including risk assessment, rapid response and coordination of risk assessment, and emergency management. The decision of the National Security and Defense Council of Ukraine dated January 25, 2015 "On the establishment and organization of the work of the Main Situational Center of Ukraine" [92] authorized the NSDC Apparatus of Ukraine to create, and organize the work of the Main Situational Center of Ukraine, as well as to collect, compile, and program an agency for business and decision-making in the field of national security and defense. According to this agency, the Main Situation Center of Ukraine should receive information from the Ministry of Defense of Ukraine, the Ministry of Internal Affairs of Ukraine, the Ministry of Foreign Affairs of Ukraine, the State Emergency Service of Ukraine, the State Emergency Service of Ukraine, the Administration of the State Border Service of Ukraine, executive authorities, other central authorities of the Republic of Tatarstan, the Security Service of Ukraine, and the Intelligence Service of Ukraine. At the stage of creating the Main Situation Center in Ukraine, certain difficulties arose in the field of information analysis, methods of its analysis, and the development of analytical models. This issue, in particular, was paid attention to by Domarev [14]. To a large extent, this situation arose due to the poor-quality of the legal infrastructure, such as the "software and technical complex" of the Main Security Center of Ukraine. In view of this, the Main Situation Center of Ukraine did not carry out assessment, analysis, notification, forecasting and modeling, early warning, and other activities that were carried out by the corresponding activities in developing countries, and needed significant reforms. Among other problems, the problems of individual strategic, organizational and legal characteristics have significantly complicated the development and implementation of universal protocols for responding to threats and crisis situations that require multiple responses to threats. In June 2021, the National Security and Defense Council of Ukraine adopted a resolution on the development of a network of situational centers, including to increase reliability, implement modern digital technologies, increase backup capabilities, establish information exchange, ensure cybersecurity and information to strengthen the business, define defense, etc. According to this decision of the SBU, the network of broad scientific centers included the Main Scientific Center of Ukraine, the Government Scientific Center, the Scientific Center of Security and Defense Sector Workers, the Scientific Center of Central Security Forces, the Ministry of the Autonomous People's Republic of Crimea, regional, state administrations of the cities of Kyiv and Sevastopol, as well as security and mobile situational centers. Analyzing the content of the measures taken through the private article, it can be concluded that they concern both network security and national stability in general, especially from the point of view of public administration policies to ensure financial reliability and transparency, as well as the situation of states of war, famine and emergencies that threaten national security Ukraine.

These difficulties do not contribute to the formation of a coherent state policy toward ensuring national peace and stability, which is based on the results of a comprehensive concept of necessity, force, coercion and vulnerability based on the jurisdiction of the state.

4.3.5. Problems of ensuring martial law in regions and territorial communities in Ukraine

The local authorities are responsible for coordination of activities and measures in the field of security at the regional and local levels, including responding to threats and emergencies, preventing them, ensuring the readiness of the state and society, responding to emergencies at the regional and local levels [12]. In general, such measures are based on national sovereignty, civil rights and special legal procedures in Ukraine and on the basis of international law, and international law is implemented. Ukrainian law regulates certain aspects of health and security measures at different levels of national security at the national and regional levels. Currently, the main role in ensuring preparedness in the regions is played by regional and district state administrations, autonomous organizations of each region (AUT), security and defense forces, emergency medical services as part of the nationwide established system, etc. In the field of prevention and response to emergency threats and extremism, the laws of Ukraine, at the territory and at the local level, have established permanent or temporary institutions, in particular: regional and local commissions on technogenic impact and the Commission on Environmental Protection and Environmental Quality Standards of Industry, Institutions and Labor; a special commission on emergency response; Coordination Group of the Anti-Terrorism Center in the SBU Regions; City Defense Center, etc.

An important step in ensuring emergency preparedness and response on the ground is the involvement of citizens in a number of measures, which include the decentralization of power in Ukraine, reform of the State Emergency Service system, and the transfer of powers in Ukraine. There are different degrees of responsibility for emergency response from state bodies to local self-government bodies. Such centers combine fire and emergency response, public safety and emergency response with a communications center and a dispatch center to coordinate activities. To create and sustain such investments in infrastructure in the security sector, it is important to coordinate efforts at the local level in the future to ensure a rapid and effective solution. In addition to the immediate response during emergencies, the city response team is called upon to assist the community, especially through information work.

A study of the current state of affairs in the implementation of interventions at the regional and local levels reveals some major problems and obstacles in establishing land stability and the stability of land communities. Measures to ensure regional and regional stability in Ukraine are fragmented and uncoordinated. The uncertainty of intellectual and institutional resources in the field of ensuring national stability has led to inconsistency in the formulation of the main goals and objectives in the field of regional and regional stability.

In particular, the Strategy of the State Regional Industrial Strategy for 2021–2027 is based on Strategic Plan 1 (Annex 2 to the Strategic Plan) [43]. At the same time, the Strategy does not address the criteria for adopting such legislation. The concept of the National Security System was tested in Ukraine only a year later. At the same time, the state strategy defines, among other things, a number of measures that can be taken to strengthen regional stability and regional independence, especially regarding their institutions (coordinated centers, regional defense forces, law enforcement and crime prevention), the creation of necessary reserves, infrastructure for protecting critical facilities, and the creation of a system for alerting the population about medical or emergency situations.

Currently, there is no mechanism for assessing risks and opportunities at the basic level. In addition, the articles rarely mention the goals and strategies for strengthening their security and sustainability. related to regional culture. The lack of a strategic vision for the development of security policies at the regional and local levels, the presence of challenges in the infrastructure and infrastructure of such initiatives – these factors create and socialize the risks of addressing the challenges of preparing for challenges is often interdisciplinary or hybrid in nature, which can lead to multiple-vectors, with cascading disclosures in different directions. The widespread development of disaster management and risk management mechanisms at the territorial level reduces attention to responding to poverty and disasters, which should be directly at the source of their occurrence. There are several difficulties in developing and implementing various national policies to ensure national security and stability at the regional level. First, there are numerous restrictions on the formation and functioning of each of the indigenous cultures and related sources, both technogenic and environmental – these are regulatory and local agricultural and agricultural commissions.

It should be noted that the ATC coordination group under the regional administration of the SBU is formed only at the regional level and in the city of Kyiv. At the same time, the relations of these groups with the district state administration, regional tribal and local authorities, as well as the local commission for the protection of the technogenic and natural environment and emergencies are not clearly defined. Thirdly, in view of the various difficulties associated with effective intervention, the concept [95] of this intervention and the action plan for the implementation of the concept [48] were developed and adopted.

The incompleteness of reforms regarding the decentralization of power creates challenges for the fair provision of public services and complicates the processes of building regional potential and increasing professional potential, as well as the direction of ensuring their integrity and sustainability. According to experts from the National Institute for Strategic Studies, this is due, in particular, to the presence of certain difficulties regarding the distribution of functions and responsibilities, regarding territorial jurisdiction and territorial integrity [21]. On the other hand, the coronavirus crisis has become an obstacle to the implementation of the decentralization process, which has made the communications necessary for decision-making in this area more important

[16]. All of the above gives grounds to state that the development of technologies is important for the creation of high-quality products and the development of cultural heritage and the development of cultural heritage.

Conclusions to the fourth chapter

A continuous analysis of current trends in global security and development models provides grounds for a more comprehensive approach. Hybrid threats have become widespread, which have a long history with nonlinear consequences. The changes taking place in the modern world disrupt many existing connections, expanding the framework of the superficial for most issues of public relations. In the long term, the security situation in Ukraine will have a broader impact on the global financial situation. The greatest long-term risk for Ukraine is the continuation of hybrid aggression by the Russian Federation, which extends to all areas of activity. Considering that the existing and potential challenges and challenges in Ukraine are of a serious, long-term nature and are a source of possible negative consequences for society and the state, which therefore require a comprehensive solution, as well as, taking into account the existing structures, states and societies and their underlying factors, which can worsen the situation (lack of reforms, limited infrastructure, difficult demographic and social conditions, etc.), it is worth mentioning that the creation of means of ensuring national stability meets the needs of Ukraine as a means of creating the possibility of ensuring national stability. The analysis conducted in the field of national security, crisis management, and consolidation of democratic governance in Ukraine allows us to conclude that the measures currently used to ensure national stability cause disagreements and instability and are therefore premature. Underdeveloped specialized legislation, as well as inadequate institutional mechanisms and mechanisms of national stabilization undermine the basic principles of national stability. In addition, the systemic process of ensuring national stability in Ukraine is obscured by the widespread lack of theoretical research on the relevant issues.

Conclusions

1. The development of agricultural policy focused on sustainable development and its dissemination throughout the supply chain is the result of the interaction and complementarity of many disciplines. At the same time, the growth of interest in national research on sustainable development indicates an active search for new tools and techniques that respond to modern challenges. Highlighting the importance of the interdisciplinary concept of sustainability, including the interdisciplinary nature of approaches and approaches, as well as the national context, to develop and deepen existing scientific research, ensuring national stability to develop a general theoretical basis for studying the field of national security, the strategies of target actors to characterize stability trends (albeit at different levels and levels), to clarify and determine the specifics of using hierarchical-conceptual approaches in the study of various aspects of policy formation in ensuring national stability.

A systemic approach to the analysis of issues of ensuring national stability was used to define the terms of formal "national development," in any shape and form – this work – considers an alternative approach to confronting pressure and problematic trends of culture, and also highlights key challenges based on the author's ideas about education in national stability.

2. Through the analysis and synthesis of scientific research on complex systems, national contexts and sustainable development, it was confirmed that the main elements of ensuring national stability are the state and society. The task of local interactions is to strengthen the stability of the state and society to an optimal level at a sufficiently high natural level, which is a higher value of the alternative knowledge base than its existing analogues for preservation.

In addition, the need to create policies to ensure the integration of national security policies in the context of poor and inclusive health systems, as well as to support for national policies for the development and implementation of these policies, requires compliance with the conditions of preservation. It was found that through the combination of these systems, a synergistic effect can be achieved. The combination of the above factors has proven its contribution to ensuring national security and stability.

3. The study of the main components of the system and the configuration of the connection and activities in the field of ensuring national stability allowed us to identify and stabilize the cycle of necessary education, which is an extension of national stability issues. This will allow us to effectively confront any technical and economic threats, adapt to changes in the security environment, and ensure the functioning of the main sectors of society and the state, which is very important for achieving sustainable development. The value, or the usefulness, of establishing a cycle of ensuring national stability is that it can be applied to the process of forming a system for ensuring national stability with its key actors and constitutional state policies for directing the works of nature.

The study of criteria, indicators, levels of ensuring national stability and risk management mechanisms turned out to be useful in the context of a changing security environment. The general interdisciplinary nature of the procedure for document circulation on issues of national stability according to the proposed methodological recommendations should lead to the development of specific methodological recommendations and indicators for the development of specific methodological recommendations on its basis and in separate areas of scientific assessment.

4. In addition, it was possible to establish the construction of a general multidimensional model of national stability using a systematic approach to the analysis of national stability, the relationships between them, factors affecting the development process, as well as from the point of view of security from a policy point of view, and also to formulate and implement an intellectual basis, guiding principles, and universal procedures for this model. The practical significance of this proposal is that on the basis of the proposed universal model and established principles, it is possible to develop a means of ensuring the national status of the state from the point of view of national security and development.

It has been scientifically proven that to ensure national stability, forces and measures to effectively respond to multidimensional threats and crisis situations are important at all levels of the national stability circle.

It has also been proved that many approaches to ensuring democratic transition are most effective in countries with a large territory and population, including Ukraine. This is due to the need for an effective first response to local and regional threats and unpleasant situations, as well as the importance of establishing reliable regional and regional systemic connections.

5. The principles identified as a result of the study of theoretical approaches to ensuring national stability are specific to the construction and functioning of an international regime in the direction of national security and stability, introduce various perspectives and concepts, especially the use of adaptive management, identification of risks and opportunities, problematic threats and vulnerabilities, strategic analysis and planning, operations development of action plans and protocols, evaluation of the lessons learned, identification of measures to ensure the resilience of communities and local communities, as well as sustainability (areas) in certain sectors, particularly on stability, including the ability to adapt to changes over time, the national stability of general and individual strategies in the implementation of target guidelines and the relevance of relevant state policies.

The results of the study of strategies for ensuring national stability may reflect the redistribution of powers between central and local authorities in the field of national stability and stabilization. At the same time, appropriate resources are needed at the regional and local levels. This, in particular, means building or strengthening regional defense capabilities, establishing reliable systemic ties based on greater cooperation, increasing social capital, etc.

It has been proven that in the direction of ensuring national stability, it is necessary to facilitate the daily activities of state authorities and local self-government bodies in implementing the priorities and programs necessary for the state, build social solidarity and solidarity in society, as well as trust in government, mainly by establishing reliable two-way communication channels between government and individuals, creating a certain moral security in the state and society, etc.

6. The results of the current analysis and generalization of foreign experience in ensuring stability in the security sphere are sufficient to assert that there is no single rule in this area. Temporary national stability is the sphere of competence of states, therefore they themselves must define the goals, objectives and set priorities for their country.

At the same time, the elements of the system and mechanisms of various states, their alliances and international organizations in their role in ensuring international stability largely relate to the concept of stability in the sphere of international relations and the related norms based on necessity.

Glossary

Adaptability is the ability of the state and society to resist destructive influences, adapt to changes in the security environment through the implementation of certain internal changes, which makes it possible to maintain integrity and continue to perform its functions.

A global risk is an event that causes a significant negative impact on several countries and industries.

Readiness is the ability of the state and society to respond quickly and appropriately to threats and crisis situations.

A threat is a potential cause of an unwanted incident that can cause harm to individuals, assets, a system or organization, the environment, or society [262].

Threats of the hybrid type are a type of threat to national security that is the result of a synergistic effect from the simultaneous use of traditional and non-traditional methods of influence and which often have a hidden nature or are disguised as other processes within the legal field.

A crisis situation is a state characterized by extreme aggravation of contradictions, significant destabilization of the situation in any field of activity, region, state, including a significant violation of the conditions of functioning of the main spheres of life society and the state, and requires taking a set of measures to stabilize the situation and restore the quality of life of the population, conditions of functioning of society and the state at a level not lower than the pre-crisis level. One of the prerequisites for the development of a crisis situation can be the emergence of an emergency situation.

Mechanisms for ensuring national stability are sets of decisions and measures that determine the sequence of certain processes, actions that correspond to the general goals and principles of functioning of the system for ensuring national stability and oriented toward the achievement of the established level and criteria by the state and society and their individual components stability

National security is the protection of national interests and national values from external and internal threats.

National stability is the ability of the state and society to effectively resist threats of any origin and nature, to adapt to changes in the security environment, to maintain stable functioning, in-

cluding during crises, to quickly recover after crises to optimal
conditions equilibrium level.

Martial law in Ukraine refers to how, in Ukraine, martial law
is defined as a special legal regime introduced in the event of
a threat of attack. The introduction of martial law is proposed by
the NSDC, approved by the president, and approved by a decision
of the Verkhovna Rada of Ukraine. Martial law was first imposed
in Ukraine in 2018, for 30 days, after Russia's first open act of aggression under its flag. After the start of the full-scale invasion,
Ukraine imposed martial law throughout the territory under its
control.

Bibliography

1. Analitychna dopovid' do shchorichnoho Poslannya Prezydenta
    Ukrayiny do Verkhovnoyi Rady Ukrayiny «Pro vnutrishnye ta
    zovnishnye stanovyshche Ukrayiny». Kyyiv: NISD, 2020. <https://
    niss.gov.ua/publikatsiyi/poslannya-prezydenta-ukrayiny/anali-
    tychna-dopovid-do-shchorichnoho-poslannya-0>

2. Abel T., & Stepp J. R. A new ecosystems ecology for anthropol-
    ogy. Conservation Ecology. 2003. Vol. 7(3). Art. 12. <https://ecolo-
    gyandsociety.org/vol7/iss3/art12/>

3. Ackoff R. Towards a system of systems concepts. Management
    Science. 1971. Vol. 17(11). Pp. 661–671. URL: https://ackoffcenter.
    blogs.com/ackoff_center_weblog/files/AckoffSystemOfSys-
    tems.pdf>

4. Adger W. N. Social and ecological resilience: Are they relat-
    ed? Progress in Human Geography. 2000. Vol. 24. Pp. 347–364.
    <https://journals.sagepub.com/toc/phgb/24/3>

5. Adger W. N., Hughes T. P., Folke C., Carpenter S. R., & Rock-
    ström J. Socialecological resilience to coastal disasters. Science.
    2005. Vol. 309. Pp. 1036– 1039. <https://science.sciencemag.org/
    content/309/5737/1036>

6. Balzacq T. The three faces of securitization: Political agency,
    audience and context. European Journal of International Re-
    lations. 2005. Vol. 11(2). Pp. 171–201. <https://journals.sagepub.
    com/doi/10.1177/1354066105052960>

7. Barrett C. B., & Constas M. A. Toward a theory of resilience for
    international development applications. Proceedings of the Na-
    tional Academy of Sciences of the USA. 2014. Vol. 111. Pp. 14625–
    14630. <https://www.pnas.org/doi/10.1073/pnas.1320880111>

8. Berkes F. Understanding uncertainty and reducing vulnerabil-
    ity: Lessons from resilience thinking. Natural Hazards. 2007.
    Vol. 41. Pp. 283–295. <https://link.springer.com/article/10.1007/
    s11069-006-9036-7>

9. Berkes F., Colding J., & Folke C. Navigating social-ecological
    systems: Building resilience for complexity and change. Cam-
    bridge: Cambridge University Press, 2003. 393 p. <http://assets.
    cambridge.org/052181/5924/sample/0521815924ws.pdf>

10. Berkes F., & Ross H. Community resilience: Toward an inte-
    grated approach. Society & Natural Resources. 2013. Vol. 26. Pp.
    5–20. <https://www.tandfonline.com/doi/abs/10.1080/08941920.2
    012.736605>

11. Bohdanovych V. Yu., Semenchenko A. I., & Yezheev M. F. Meth-
    ods of state management of ensuring national security in its
    determining areas: Education manual Kyiv: NADU, 2008. 40 p.

12. Buzan B., & Waever O. Security: A new framework for analysis. Boulder: Lynne, 1998. 239 p.

13. BOHÁČ, Vojtěch. Všechny cesty vedou k válce: Příběh Ruska a Ukrajiny očima českého reportéra 2011-2022. 1. Praha: Cpress, 2022. ISBN 978-80-264-4527-2.

14. Glushak O. M. Experience of implementation of risk-oriented planning and safety culture in bodies and units of the national police of Ukraine. Development of civil protection in modern security conditions: the mother 21 All-Ukrainian science and practice conf. (with international participation) (Kyiv, October 8 2019). Electr. kind. Kyiv: IDUCZ, 2019. 328 p. P. 68–75.

15. Čermák, Petr a Dana Čermáková. Volodymyr Zelenskyj: Duši i tělo za svobodu. 1. 2022. ISBN 978-80-88471-09-7. [3] Dějiny Ukrajiny / Jan Rychlík, Bohdan Zilynskyj, Paul Robert Magocsi. Praha: NLN, 2022 . 527 stran ilustrace, mapy, portréty, faksimile, erby; ISBN 978-80-7422-849-0

16. Chandler D. Beyond neoliberalism: Resilience, the new art of governing complexity. Resilience. 2014. Vol. 2(1). Pp. 47–63.

17. Chandler D. Resilience and human security: The post-interventionist paradigm. Security Dialogue. 2012. Vol. 43(3). p. 213–229.

18. Churchman C. W., Ratoosh P. (Eds.). Measurement: Definitions and theories. New York: John Wiley, 1959. 64 p.

19. Corning P. A. The Re-Emergence of "Emergence": A Venerable Concept in Search of a Theory. Complexity. 2002. Vol. 7(6). Pp. 18–30. <https://onlinelibrary.wiley.com/doi/epdf/10.1002/cplx.10043>

20. Council of Australian Governments. Australia's Counter-Terrorism Strategy. Strengthening Our Resilience. <https://www.nationalsecurity.gov.au/what-australia-is-doing-subsite/Files/australias-counter-terrorism-strategy-2015.pdf>

21. Council of the European Union. Council Conclusions on EU Approach to Resilience. Brussels. 28 May 2013. <https://www.consilium.europa.eu/uedocs/cms_data/docs/pressdata/en/foraff/137319.pdf>

22. Council of the European Union. European Security Strategy. A Secure Europe in a Better World. <https://www.consilium.europa.eu/en/resources/publications/european-security-strategy-secure-europe-better-world/>

23. Council of the European Union. Implementation Plan on Security and Defence. 14 November 2016. <https://www.consilium.europa.eu/media/22460/eugs-implementation-plan-st14392en16.pdf>

24. Council of the European Union. Proposal for a Regulation of the European Parliament and of the Council establishing a Recovery and Resilience Facility. (2020/0104 (COD)). Brussels. 21 December 2020. <https://eur-lex.europa.eu/legal-content/EN/TXT/?uri=CELEX:52020PC0408>

25. Crane T. A. Of models and meanings: Cultural resilience in socialecological systems. Ecology and Society. 2010. Vol. 15(4). Art. 19. <https://ecologyandsociety.org/vol15/iss4/art19/>

26. Curtin C. G., & Parker J. P. Foundations of resilience thinking. Conservation Biology. 2014. Vol. 28. Pp. 912–923. <https://conbio.onlinelibrary.wiley.com/doi/abs/10.1111/cobi.12321>

27. Definitions of Community Resilience: An Analysis: A CARRI Report. Community and Regional Resilience Institute, 2013. <https://zcralliance.org/resources/item/definitions-of-community-resilience-an-analysis/>

28. Deterring Terror. How Israel Confronts the Next Generation of Threats. Belfer Center Special Report 2016. English Translation of the Official Strategy of the Israel Defense Forces. Fareword by Graham Allison / Belfer Center for Science and International Affairs. 62 p.

29. Dillon M., & Neal A. (Eds.) Foucault on politics, security and war. Palgrave Macmillan, 2008. 252 p. <https://www.researchgate.net/profile/AndrewNeal/publication/267206491_Foucault_on_Politics_Security_and_War/links/54e39d060cf2b2314f5de23b/Foucault-on-PoliticsSecurity-and-War.pdf> (дата звернення: 17.08.2021).

30. Donno R. Building national resilience: Survive crisis, seize opportunity, prepare for change. Booz Allen Hamilton, Inc., 2017.

31. Domarev V. V. The situational management system: Theory, methodology, recommendations Kyiv: Knowledge of Ukraine, 2017. 347 p.

32. Donbas and Crimea: The price of return: A monograph [in general ed. V. P. Horbulina, O. S. Vlasyuk, E. M. Libanova, O. M. Lyashenko]. Kyiv: NISD, 2015. P. 181–191.

33. Eisenkot G., & Siboni G. Guidelines for Israel's National Security Strategy. The Washington Institute for Near East Policy, 2019. 73 p.

34. European Commission. Action Plan on the Sendai Framework for Disaster Risk Reduction 2015–2030. A disaster risk-informed approach for all EU policies. Commission staff working document. SWD(2016)205final/2. Brussels, 2016. 17 June. <https://eur-lex.europa.eu/legal-content/EN/TXT/PDF/?uri=CELEX:52016AR5035>

35. European Commission. Building resilience: The EU's approach. <https://ec.europa.eu/echo/files/aid/countries/factsheets/thematic/EU_building_resilience_en.pdf>

36. European Commission. Building resilience: The EU's approach. Factsheet. <https://ec.europa.eu/echo/files/aid/countries/factsheets/thematic/EU_building_resilience_en.pdf>

37. European Commission. Commission staff working document guidance to member states recovery and resilience plans. SWD(2021)12final. Brussels, 2021. 22 Jan. <https://ec.europa.eu/info/sites/default/files/document_travail_service_part1_v2_en.pdf>

38. European Commission. Communication from the Commission to the European Parliament and the Council. The EU approach to resilience: Learning from food security crises. Brussels, 2012. 03 Oct. <https://eur-lex.europa.eu/legal-content/EN/TXT/?uri=celex:52012DC0586>

39. European Commission. Communication to the European Parliament, the Council, the European Economic and Social Committee and the Committee of the Regions. Tackling online disinformation: A European Approach. COM(2018)236final. Brussels, 2018. 26 Apr. <https://eurlex.europa.eu/legal-content/EN/TXT/?uri=CELEX:52018DC0236>

40. European Commission. Joint framework on countering hybrid threats: A European Union response. Joint Communication to the European Parliament 18final. Brussels, 2016. 06 Apr. <https://eur-lex.europa.eu/legal-content/EN/TXT/?uri=celex:52016JC0018>

41. European Commission. The EU approach to resilience: Learning from food security crises. Factsheet. <https://ec.europa.eu/echo/files/aid/countries/factsheets/thematic/resilience_africa_en.pdf>

42. European Council. Joint statement of the members of the European Council. Brussels, 2020. 26 March. <https://www.consilium.europa.eu/en/press/press-releases/2020/03/26/joint-statement-of-the-members-of-the-european-council-26-march-2020/>

43. European Council. Council Regulation concerning humanitarian aid (EC) No 1257/96 of 20 June 1996. Official Journal of the European Union. 1996. 02 July. <https://eur-lex.europa.eu/legal-content/EN/TXT/PDF/?uri= CELEX:31996R1257&from=EN>

44. European Council. Council Regulation on the provision of emergency support within the Union. 2016/369 of 15 March 2016. Official Journal of the European Union. 2016. 16 March. <https://

eur-lex.europa.eu/ legal-content/EN/TXT/PDF/?uri=CELEX:320
16R0369&from=EN>

45. European Council. Roadmap for recovery. Towards a more
resilient, sustainable and fair Europe. 2020. 5 p. <https://www.
consilium.europa.eu/media/43384/roadmap-for-recovery-fi-
nal-21-04-2020.pdf>

46. European Parliament and Council. Decision No 1313/2013/EU
of the European Parliament and of the Council on a Union Civil
Protection Mechanism. 17 December 2013. Official Journal of
the European Union. 2013. 20 Dec. <https://eur-lex.europa.eu/
eli/dec/2013/1313/oj/eng>

47. European Parliament and Council. Regulation (EU) 2021/241
of the European Parliament and of the Council of 12 February
2021 establishing the Recovery and Resilience Facility. Official
Journal of the European Union. 2021. 18 Feb. <https://eur-lex.eu-
ropa.eu/legal-content/EN/TXT/PDF/?uri=CELEX:32021R0241&f
rom=EN>

48. European Parliament and Council. Regulation (EU) 2021/888
establishing the European Solidarity Corps Programme and
repealing Regulations (EU) 2018/1475 and (EU) No 375/2014. Official Journal of the European Ольга, June. <https://eur-lex.eu-
ropa.eu/legal-content/ EN/TXT/PDF/?uri=CELEX:32021R0888&
from=en>

49. European Parliament. Resilience as a Strategic Priority of the
External Action of the EU. Resolution 2017/2594(RSP). Brussels,
2017. 01 June. <https://eur-lex.europa.eu/legal-content/EN/TXT/
PDF/?uri=CELEX:52017IP0242>

50. European Union. Treaty of Lisbon. Amending the Treaty on European Union and the Treaty establishing the European Community. Signed at Lisbon, 13 December 2007. Official Journal
of the European Union. 2007. 17 Dec. <https://eur-lex.europa.eu/
eli/treaty/lis/sign/eng>

51. European Union. A Global Strategy for the European
Union's Foreign and Security Policy. Shared Vision, Common
Action: A Stronger Europe. <https://www.eeas.europa.eu/sites/
default/files/eugs_review_web_0.pdf>

52. Evans B., & Reid J. Exhausted by resilience: Response to the
commentaries. Resilience. 2015. Vol. 3(2). Pp. 154–159.

53. Jones R. W. Security, strategy and critical theory. London: Lynne
Rienner Publishers, 1999. 196 p.

54. Fiksel J. Designing resilient, sustainable systems. Environmental Science and Technology. 2003. Vol. 37(23). Pp. 5330–5339. <https://pubs.acs.org/doi/10.1021/es0344819>

55. Fjäder C. The nation-state, national security and resilience in the age of globalization. Resilience. 2014. Vol. 2(2). Pp. 114–129.

56. Fenwick, Gallagher. Volodymyr Zelenskyj: Ukrajina v krvi. Překlad Zuzana RAKOVÁ. První vydání. Praha: Euromedia Group, 2022. 212 stran. Universum. ISBN 978-80-242-8343- 2.

57. Gavora P. Úvod do pedagogického výzkumu. Brno: Paido, 2010. 2. vyd. ISBN 978– 80-7315-185-0.

58. Hendl, J. K. & Hendl, J. Kvalitativní výzkum: základní teorie, metody a aplikace. 2. aktualiz. vyd. Praha: Portál, 2008. 407 s. ISBN 978-80-7367-485-4.

59. Holling C. S. Adaptive environmental assessment and management. London: Wiley, 1978. 377 p.

60. Holling C. S. Resilience and stability of ecological systems. Annual Review of Ecology and Systematics. 1973. Vol. 4. Pp. 1–23.

61. Holling C. S. Understanding the complexity of economic, ecological, and social systems. Ecosystem. 2001. Vol. 4. Pp. 390–405.

62. Hovory o Ukrajině / Radomyr Mokryk odpovídá na otázky Jiřího Padevěta. Praha Academia, 2023. 190 stran. ISBN 978-80-200-3436-6.

63. Horbulin V. P., & Kachynskyi A. B. Strategic planning: Solution problems of national security. Kyiv: NISD, 2010. 288 p.

64. Horbulin V. P., Kachynskyi A. B. Fundamentals of national security of Ukraine. Kyiv: Intertehnologiya, 2009. 272 p.

65. Zhalilo Ya. A., Bazylyuk Ya. B., Kovalivska S. V., Kolomiets O. O. and others. Ukraine after the corona crisis - the path to recovery: science. add. Kyiv: NISD, 2020. 304 p. <https://niss.gov.ua/sites/default/files/2020-11/ukraina-pislya-koronakrizi_sait.pdf>

66. Haydanka Y., Martinkovič M. Decentralization and electoral processes: Political fragmentation of the regions in the Czech Republic. Typi Universitatis Tyrnaviensis and VEDA. TRNAVA 2022. 118 p.

67. Horký, Petr. Ukrajina: Rozhovory, Mýta a Fakta. 1. Praha: Cpress, 2022. ISBN 978-80- 264-4356-8.

68. Held D., McGrew A. The end of the old order? Globalization and the prospects for World order. Review of International Studies. 1998. Vol. 24. No. 4. Pp. 219–245.

69. Kaczynskii A. B. Indicator of power as an integral indicator state security. Mathematical Modeling in Economics. 2015. Vol. 2. C. 75–91.

70. Kovalivska S. V. Coordination of actions of local executive bodies and local self-government bodies in the field of anti-epidemic measures: Analyst. zap Kyiv: NISD, 2020. <https://niss.gov.ua/sites/default/files/2020-08/mistsevi-organy-covid_0.pdf>

71. Kovalivska S. V., Barynova D. S., & Nesterenko V. V. About risks for proper provision of public services in connection with changes in the administrative and territorial system of Ukraine: Analyst. zap Kyiv: NISD, 2020. <https://niss.gov.ua/sites/default/files/2020-10/publichni-poslugy-1.pdf>

72. Kornievsky O. National security. Political encyclopedia / editor: Yu. Levenets (head), Yu. Shapoval (deputy head). Kyiv: Parliamentary Publishing House, 2011. 808 p. P. 489–490.

73. Křížek Z. Cesta z Ruska: Ruská agrese proti Ukrajině a její důsledky. 1. Brno: Masarikova Univerzita, 2023. P. 120

74. Lasconjarias G. Deterrence through Resilience. NATO, the nations and the challenges of being prepared / research division – NATO Defense College, Rome. Eisenhower Paper. 2017. Vol. 7. Pp. 1–8.

75. Marchuk V. Ukraine's European integration in the political dimension of Central and Eastern Europe. Trnava: Typi Universitatis Tyrnaviensis; Praha: Academia, 2022. 92 p.

76. Marchuk V., & Dudkevych, V. European integration of Ukraine: Political and security practices. Typi Universitatis Tyrnaviensis and VEDA. TRNAVA 2022. 144 p.

77. Marchuk V., & Dudkevych, V. European Integration of Ukraine: Political and Security Practices. Typi Universitatis Tyrnaviensis, spoločné pracovisko Trnavskej univerzity v Trnave a Vedy, vydavateľstva Slovenskej akadémie vied, 144 p. 2022. ISBN: 978-80-568-0504-61.

78. Marchuk V., Pavlova L., Ahafonova H., Vonsovych S., & Simonian, A. Communication opportunities of civil society institutions in countering the challenges of post-pandemic postmodernity. Postmodern Openings. 2021. Vol. 12(1Sup1), Pp. 335–345.

79. Marchuk V. V., & Holubiyak N. R. Diplomatic personnel training in the context of formation and development of Czech Diplomacy (1989–2004). Actual Problems of Philosophy and Sociology. Vol. 41. Odesa: "Helvetika" Publishing House 2023. Pp. 141–145.

80. Marples, D. The war in Ukraine's Donbas: Origins, contexts, and the future. Central European University Press, 2022. ISBN 978-9633864197.

81. Mladá fronta dnes: Kyberútok na Česko jako ruská pomsta. Praha: MAFRA, 2023. ISSN 12101168.

82. Mrštík, V. Cesta do Ruska: listy z Nižního Novgorodu 1896. Praha: Arkýř, 1992. 159 s. ISBN 80-85400-01-4.

83. North Atlantic Treaty. Washington, DC, April 4, 1949 <https://www.nato.int/cps/uk/natohq/official_texts_17120. htm?selectedLocale=en>

84. The President approved the plan for the admission of foreign military personnel to Ukraine for training in 2021. <https://www.president.gov.ua/news/prezident-zatverdiv-plan-dopusku-inozemnih-vijskovih-v-ukray-66413>

85. On the fight against terrorism: Law of Ukraine dated March 20, 2003 No. 638-IV. information of the Verkhovna Rada of Ukraine. 2003. No. 25. Art. 180.

86. On volunteering: Law of Ukraine dated April 19, 2011 No. 3236-Information of the Verkhovna Rada of Ukraine. 2011. No. 42. Art. 435.

87. On establishing security and information protection requirements for qualified providers of electronic trust services and their separate registration points: Order of the Administration of the State Service for Special Communications and Information Protection of Ukraine dated 05/14/2020 No. 269. <https://zakon.rada.gov.ua/laws/show/z0668-20#Text>

88. On public-private partnership: Law of Ukraine dated July 1, 2010 No. 2404-VI. Information of the Verkhovna Rada of Ukraine. 2010. No. 40. Art. 524.

89. On emergency medical care: Law of Ukraine dated 07/05/2012 No. 5081-VI. Information of the Verkhovna Rada of Ukraine. 2013. No. 30. Art. 340.

90. On the approval of the Requirements for determining the procedure for the actions of the personnel of the physical protection division, the personnel of the division of accounting and control of nuclear materials in emergency and crisis situations: Order of the Ministry of Energy and Coal Industry of Ukraine and the Ministry of Emergency Situations of Ukraine dated September 15, 2011. No. 501/1001. <https://zakon.rada.gov.ua/laws/show/z1147-11#Text>

91. On approval of the State Regional Development Strategy for 2021–2027 Resolution of the Cabinet of Ministers of Ukraine dated 08/05/2020 No. 695. <https://zakon.rada.gov.ua/laws/show/695-2020-%D0%BF#Text>

92. On the approval of the Instructions for fighting for the survivability of inland navigation vessels: Order of the Ministry of Transport and Communications of Ukraine

93. On the approval of the Instructions for carrying out risk analysis in the State Border Service of Ukraine: Order of the Ministry of Internal Affairs of Ukraine dated 11.12.2017. No. 1007. <https://zakon.rada.gov.ua/laws/show/ z0091-18#Text>

94. On approval of the Transmission System Code: Resolution of the National commission carrying out state regulation in the spheres of energy and communal services dated March 14, 2018 No. 309. <https://zakon.rada.gov.ua/laws/show/v0309874-18#Text>

95. On the approval of normative legal acts on matters of provision emergency medical care: Order of the Ministry of Health of Ukraine dated September 24, 2020. No. 2179. <https://zakon.rada.gov.ua/laws/show/z1192-20#Text>

96. On the approval of the plan of measures for the implementation of the Concept of the development of the emergency medical care system Cabinet Order of the Ministers of Ukraine dated January 29, 2020. No. 111. <https://zakon.rada.gov.ua/laws/show/111-2020-%D1%80#Text>

97. On the approval of the Regulation on the unified state system of prevention, response and termination of terrorist acts and their minimization consequences: Resolution of the Cabinet of Ministers of Ukraine dated February 18, 2016. No. 92. <https://zakon.rada.gov.ua/laws/show/92-2016-п#Text>

98. On the approval of the Regulation on the unified state system of civil protection: Resolution of the Cabinet of Ministers of Ukraine dated January 9, 2014. No. 11. <https://zakon.rada.gov.ua/laws/show/11-2014-п#Text>

99. On approval of the Regulation on the Congress of local and regional authorities under the President of Ukraine: Decree of the President of Ukraine dated 03/04/2021 No. 89/2021. <https://zakon.rada.gov.ua/laws/show/89/2021#Text>

100. On the approval of the Regulations on naval service in the Naval Forces of the Armed Forces of Ukraine: Order of the Ministry of Defense of Ukraine.

101. Poselství z Kyjeva o Ukrajině a Evropě/Konstantin Sigov; překlad: Lenka Karfíková, Filip Karfík. V Praze: Bourdon, 2023. 112 stran ilustrace; ISBN 978-80-7611-073-1

102. Poselství z Ukrajiny: proslovy z let 2019–2022 / Volodymyr Zelenskyj; přeložil Viktor Janiš. Praha: Argo, 2023. 151 stran. ISBN 978-80-257-4043-9.

103. Reichel J. Kapitoly metodologie sociálních výzkumů. 1. vyd. Praha: Grada, 2009. 167 s. ISBN 978-80-247-3006-6.

104. Reznikova O. O. Conceptual approaches to the choice of a model for ensuring national stability. Strategic Priorities. 2019. Vol. 1. Pp. 18–27.

105. Reznikova O. O. Conceptual approaches to the development of an early warning system as a mechanism for ensuring national stability. Bulletin of Lviv University. Series: Philosophical and Political Science Studio. 2019. Vol. 23. Pp. 196–202.

106. Reznikova O. O. Mechanisms for ensuring the stability of the state in the sphere of national security. Strategic priorities. 2018. No. 3-4. P. 15–25. 107. Reznikova O. O. Peculiarities of the formation of state policy according to principles of national stability. Bulletin of Lviv University. Series: Philosophical and Political Studies. 2018. No. 18. C. 349–353.

107. Reznikova O. O. Passport of the separatist threat in Ukraine. Strategic priorities. 2018. No. 2. P. 12–24.

108. River C. Modern Ukraine: The history of the country since the 20th century. 2020. ISBN 9781094279732.

109. Sytnyk G. P., Abramov V. I., Mandragelya V. A. and others. Justification conceptual and organizational and legal basis for the development of passports of threats to the national security of Ukraine: teaching method. manual / under the editorship G. P. Sytnyk. Kyiv: NADU, 2012. 52 p.

110. Sytnyk G. P. Conceptual principles of ensuring national security of Ukraine: Training. manual: in 3 h. Kyiv: NADU, 2010. Part 3: State policy and fundamentals of strategic planning for ensuring national security. 208 p.

111. Sytnyk G. P. National security. Encyclopedia of public administration: in 8 vols. Kyiv: NADU, 2011. Vol. 1. 748 p.

112. Yu. M. Skaletskyi, D. S. Biryukov, O. O. Martyusheva, and YatsenkoL. D.. Problems of implementing safety culture in Ukraine: analyst. add. Kyiv: NISD, 2012. 17 p. <https://niss.gov.ua/doslidzhennya/nacionalna-bezpeka/problemi-vprovadzhennya-kulturi-bezpeki-v-ukraini-analitichna>

113. Tama J. Why Strategic Planning Matters to National Security. Lawfare. 2016. 6 Mar. <https://www.lawfaremedia.org/article/why-strategic-planning-matters-national-security>

114. Thompson E. P. Beyond the cold war. London: Merlin Press, 1982. 36 p.

115. Ullman R. Redefining Security. International Security. 1983. Vol. 8(1). Pp. 129–153.

116. Walker J., & Cooper M. Genealogies of resilience: From systems ecology to the political economy of crisis adaptation. Security Dialogue. 2011. Vol. 42(2). Pp. 143–160.

117. Walklate S., McGarry R., & Mythen G. Searching for resilience: A conceptual excavation. Armed Forces & Society. 2013. Vol. 40(3). Pp. 408–427.

118. Welfens, P. Russia's invasion of Ukraine: Economic challenges, embargo issues and a new global economic order. 1. Germany: Springer International Publishing, 2023. ISBN 978-3-031-19137-4.

www.ingramcontent.com/pod-product-compliance
Lightning Source LLC
Chambersburg PA
CBHW071747270326
41928CB00013B/2830